MODERN COMBAT HELICOPTERS

MILITARY AIRCRAFT

▌▌▌▌▌▌▌▌▌▌▌▌▌▌▌▌▌▌▌▌▌▌▌▌▌▌▌▌

MODERN COMBAT HELICOPTERS

George Sullivan

 Facts On File

New York

MODERN COMBAT HELICOPTERS

Copyright © 1993 by George Sullivan

Facts On File, Inc.
460 Park Avenue South
New York NY 10016

Library of Congress Cataloging-in-Publication Data

Sullivan, George.
  Modern combat helicopters / George Sullivan.
    p.   cm. — (Military aircraft)
  Includes index.
  Summary: Profiles thirteen of the world's most widely used combat helicopters, including the AH-64 Apache, the Bell AH-1 Cobra, and the UH-60 Black Hawk.
   ISBN 0-8160-2353-0
   1. Military helicopters—Juvenile literature. [1. Military
UG1230.S85   1993
358.4'183—dc2092-314392

British CIP data available on request from Facts On File.

Text and cover design by Ron Monteleone
Composition by Facts On File, Inc.
Manufactured by R.R. Donnelley & Sons, Inc.
Printed in the United States of America

Front cover photo of an AH-1W helicopter, courtesy of Bell Helicopter

10 9 8 7 6 5 4 3 2 1

This book is printed on acid-free paper.

CONTENTS

ACKNOWLEDGMENTS

Many individuals contributed information and photographs for use in this book. Special thanks are due the following: Bettie Sprigg, Department of Defense; Russell D. Egnor, Department of the Navy; Larry Wilson, Dan Hagadorne and Tim Cronin, National Air and Space Museum; Maj. Mark Hughes, Lt. Mike Snider and S/Sgt. Terry Ruggles, U.S. Marine Corps; Capt. Robert Gonzales, M/Sgt. Ernest C. Dawson, U.S. Air Force; M/Sgt. Sunny Taylor, U.S. Army; Bill Tuttle, Sikorsky Aircraft; Bob Leder, Bell Helicopter Textron; Roger Torgerson, Bell/Boeing; D. M. Willis, McDonnell Douglas Helicopter Co.; David Bath, Westland Group PLC; Renato Ughi, Agusta Sp.A.; Cristina Gotzhein, Messerschmitt-Bolkow-Blohm GmbH; and Francesca Kurti, TLC Labs.

INTRODUCTION

Of all the world's flying machines, none is quite like the helicopter. It can fly up or fly down, or fly forward, backward or sideways. It can hover like a hummingbird. It can even spin around in circles.

The helicopter was first developed in 1907, just a few years after the Wright Brothers flew at Kitty Hawk. But the military potential of the aircraft helicopter wasn't fully appreciated until fairly recent times.

While some helicopters were used during World War II, chiefly in search-and-rescue missions, it was during the Korean War, from 1950 to 1953, that the helicopter's versatility was first demonstrated. Military experts came to realize that the helicopter could go places and do things that a fixed-wing aircraft could not do.

At about the same time the Korean War was being fought, engineers were adapting the jet engine for use in helicopters. This advance enabled helicopters to fly faster, go higher and carry much heavier loads than ever before. The use of helicopters grew by leaps and bounds.

The war in Vietnam (1957–1975) has been called the "Helicopter War." "They were everywhere; day or night, rain or shine, good weather or bad; they were seen or heard every hour of the day," wrote Michael Novosil in *U.S. Army Aviation Digest*. "They hauled ash and trash; engaged in combat assaults; served as weapons platforms; scouted and flushed out enemy forces; transferred the wounded from forward med-ical-aid facilities to rear-area hospitals, and went into the thick of battle to evacuate the wounded to life-saving medical care."

In every war since, helicopters have played a key role—in Afghanistan and the Falkland Islands, in Grenada and the Persian Gulf. In the major tank battle of the war in the Persian Gulf, an American Apache AH-64 was credited with destroying nine enemy tanks.

In recent years, the world of combat helicopters has gone through a period of enormous change. This is because of avionics, the electronic equipment that goes into a helicopter.

It used to be that a helicopter was purchased on the basis of its airframe and propulsion system. But by the late 1980s, helicopter manufacturers and their military customers were mostly in agreement on what these should be like and how they should perform.

The on-board electronics are what is important today. These include the flight controls and navigation equipment, the computers, the radar, sonar, and laser and infrared countermeasures.

The change that has taken place was dramatized in 1991 when the British Royal Navy awarded IBM a $2.5 billion contract to build 44 helicopters packed with electronic gear designed for antisubmarine warfare.

When you think IBM, you think computers. But now IBM is also a helicopter company.

The movie *Blue Thunder* (1983) starred an ultra-sophisticated helicopter that was used by a Los Angeles police officer to wage war against crime. The helicopter could do some pretty wild things, such as see through walls. Tomorrow's helicopters, with their advanced avionics and more powerful weapons systems, may make *Blue Thunder* seem quite normal.

1   McDONNELL DOUGLAS AH-64 APACHE

The AH-64 Apache is the newest and most potent of the Army's helicopter gunships. It bristles with missiles and rockets designed to destroy enemy tanks and other armored vehicles on the ground and to blast hostile helicopters out of the sky. To some observers, it is the toughest, most awesome helicopter ever built.

During the Persian Gulf War in 1991, Apaches were the first allied weapon to "fire shots in anger." Eight Apaches, accompanied by a Sikorsky UH-60 Black Hawk, attacked enemy early-warning radar sites deep within Iraq at 2:38 A.M. on the morning of January 17, 1991.

AH-64A APACHE FACT SHEET

Manufacturer: McDonnell Douglas Helicopter Company

Type: Advanced antitank attack helicopter

Power Plant: Two T700-GE-701 turboshafts, each delivering 1,690 horsepower

Length: 48 ft., 2 in.

Height: 15 ft., 3 in.

Maximun Takeoff Weight: 21,000 lb.

Main Rotor Diameter: 48 ft.

Crew: (2) One pilot, one copilot/gunner

First Flight: 1975

Cruising Speed: 185 mph

Range: 300 mi.

Bristling with rockets and missiles, the AH-64 Apache is the deadliest gunship ever built. (McDonnell Douglas Helicopter Company)

Operating in two teams of four aircraft each, the Apaches hit the power station supplying the radar installation first, then its communication facilities and last, the radar units themselves. The radar sites were out of action in a matter of seconds and destroyed completely in four minutes.

The attack opened up a "radar black" corridor through the ring of air defenses that surrounded Iraq, providing an airway through which allied aircraft could fly without fear of being detected. Within minutes after the raid, some 100 aircraft poured through the gap on their way to bomb the Iraqi capital of Baghdad.

The eight helicopters also carried out reconnaissance missions as part of the assault. As they flew to and from the radar sites, each helicopter used its videotape system to monitor images of other possible targets. The tapes were later evaluated by mission planners.

The AH-64 Apache dates to the mid-1970s, when the Army began seeking designs for a new attack helicopter, a two-seat aircraft that would be capable of operating day or night in all types of weather. The winning design was submitted by Hughes Helicopters (acquired by McDonnell Douglas Corporation in 1984).

As of the early 1990s, the Army had ordered a total of 807 AH-64s, of which about 650 were in operation. At one time, the McDonnell Douglas manufacturing plant in Mesa, Arizona, was turning out Apaches at the rate of ten a month. Approximately 200 AH-64s saw duty in the Persian Gulf War.

In the Apache, the pilot and copilot/gunner (CPG) are seated in separate compartments, one behind the other. This has several benefits over the old side-by-side seating. It permits a narrower fuselage, making the helicopter a more difficult target, at least from the front and rear.

First production models of the Apache were delivered to the Army in 1984. By the early 1990s, more than 800 had been produced. (U.S. Army)

It also allows the crew members to be isolated for greater safety. Each cockpit is surrounded with heavy armor plating, and the two are divided by a transparent blast shield. If one of the crew members should be hit, the chances are good the other will survive.

The aircraft's twin turbine engines also offer a safety factor. If one should be put out of operation, the other can keep the helicopter aloft.

Special filters cover the engine air intakes. These are meant to prevent sand from clogging vital parts during desert operations. (Such jamming is believed to have been a factor in the breakdown of Navy helicopters during the disastrous attempt to rescue U.S. hostages in Iran in 1980. See page 58–59.)

The Apache cruises at 185 miles an hour and has a "never exceed speed" of 229 mph. Through the use of auxiliary fuel tanks for extended range, the Apache is capable of flying across the Atlantic Ocean to Europe.

The aircraft's structural design stresses survivability. the fuel cells are self-sealing. Each of the rotor's four fiberglass blades has been fitted with a stainless steel leading edge meant to withstand tree-branch strikes or

The chief mission of the AH-64 Apache is to support troops in the field. (McDonnell Douglas Helicopter Company)

other such mishaps. The landing gear has been reinforced so as to absorb a straight-down impact of up to 20 feet per second. The helicopter's two General Electric engines are mounted 6.6 feet apart, and each is covered with armored shielding as protection against enemy ground fire.

When an Apache on a training mission at Fort Hood, Texas, struck power lines, the crew walked away from the crash. If they had been flying another helicopter, the crash might have killed them. The Apache was repaired and flying again within six months.

In the years before the breakup of the Soviet Union in 1991, the Apache was intended to meet the threat of Soviet battle tanks in a European land war. In their battle plan, called Operation Deep Strike, experts who represented the North Atlantic Treaty Organization (NATO) calculated exactly how their helicopter gunships and other weapons would cope with a Soviet invasion. Their plan took into account that Soviet troops, supported by their Warsaw Pact allies, would far outnumber the forces of NATO.

As the first wave attacked, it would be deliberately allowed to penetrate NATO lines. Once the enemy was deep inside NATO territory, a divide-and-conquer strategy would be followed in which the attackers would be encircled and defeated.

In the meantime, antitank helicopters such as the Apache, plus fixed-wing aircraft and ballistic missiles, would be used to launch a massive assault on the enemy forces still within the Soviet Union—the second and third waves of attacking troops. A force of 600 helicopter gunships, it was believed, could "kill" as many as 10,000 enemy tanks.

Of course, the collapse of the Soviet empire and the remaking of the Soviet state in 1990 and 1991 put an end to such theorizing. Yet the planning that was done goes a long way toward helping to explain the enormous firepower of the AH-64. It had a very big job to do.

The Hellfire laser-guided missile is the Apache's main antitank weapon. Supersonic and with a range of five miles, the Hellfire can be ripple-fired, meaning several missiles can be launched in quick succession toward different targets, using coded laser beams. The missiles will climb above obstacles before searching for their coded targets, homing in on them once they've been designated. The Apache carries a total of 16 Hellfires.

The Hellfire is backed up by another fearsome piece of equipment, a turret-mounted 30mm chain gun. Capable of firing 10 rounds per second, it gives the Apache the capability of not only knocking out tanks but also defending itself against enemy helicopters and even

Some armament options for the AH-64, including 1,200 rounds of 30mm ammunition, 76 unguided 2.75-inch 75mm rockets, and Hellfire antiarmor missiles. (McDonnell Douglas Helicopter Company)

fixed-wing aircraft. The gun—it's really more of a cannon than a gun—has a range of well over half a mile, meaning that it can be fired at a comfortable distance from the enemy.

When, in the mid-1970s, the Army asked aircraft manufacturers to submit designs for the attack helicopter that was to become the Apache, the Army stressed that the helicopter's weapons were to be a part of its design. What the Army didn't want was weapons that were merely add-ons. Some well-known weapons were not chosen because they were too heavy and too bulky.

The Gatling gun was one that was considered. With its rotating cluster of barrels, each barrel being automatically loaded and fired on every turn, the Gatling gun gets high marks for its reliability and rate of fire. But the Gatling gun was rejected for the Apache because of its complexity and weight.

Instead, engineers devised a single barrel gun with a rotating bolt. (The bolt is the mechanism that shoves each shell into the firing chamber.) It's called a chain gun because an electrically driven motor-cycle-type chain and sprocket drive the bolt.

In tests, the chain gun showed itself to be superior to other types of guns. It had a high performance rating, was light in weight and easy to maintain. Its streamlined design meant little wind drag, once the gun was in place beneath the fuselage.

The Army is not without experience in the operation of chain guns, incidentally. The Bushmaster, a 25mm chain gun, is the main gun on the Army's Bradley Fighting Vehicle, on the Marine Corps' Piranha, and on several other armored fighting vehicles (AFVs).

The Apache is also equipped with rocket pods that can carry a variety of warheads. The rockets can be launched as singles, in pairs or in salvos. Either the pilot or CPG can do the firing.

The "eyes" of the Apache consist of three electronic systems that, to helicopter pilots of the Vietnam era, at least, seem almost magical. They permit a pilot to see in the dark, spot targets ordinarily hidden from view, and to skim over rough terrain at tree-top level, even at night or in bad weather.

These systems are made up, first of all, of a Target Acquisition Designation Sight, or TADS. This consists of a TV camera for daylight viewing, an infrared imager for night, and a laser-beam generator for spotting targets and guiding the missiles. All the Apache's gunner has to do is aim the laser at the target, and the missile will automatically ride the beam to whatever it is pointed at.

The system also includes a Pilot Night Vision Sensor, or PNVS. This features an infrared receiver that produces an illuminated view of the terrain below at night or when the ground happens to be obscured by fog or heavy rain. With PNVS, a pilot can fly at night at very low altitudes.

The TADS/PNVS systems can be used in combination with a helmet gunsight. The sight enables the pilot or gunner to aim the scanners by simply moving his or her head. This helmet gunsight was the subject of an article in *Popular Mechanics*. The title of the article: "The Look That Kills."

The Apache is the Army's weapon, and the Army's alone. The Navy has no interest in wiping out tanks. As for the Air Force and Marine Corps, they rely on the A-10 Thunderbolt II, a fixed-wing aircraft, to provide close support for ground troops and to knock out enemy tanks and other armor.

A low-flying, slow-flying, single-seat, two-engine aircraft, able to duck around clusters of trees and low buildings, armed with a powerful 30mm Gatling gun, the A-10 has won loud praise. Not only has it proven to be an effective tank killer, it also costs less than the Apache, or about $10 million per A-10 compared to $11.7 million for an AH-64.

A major problem for the Army has been the Apache's technical complexity, which effects the aircraft's reliability. At one time, Army maintenance crews had difficulty keeping the Apache flying.

A study released by the General Accounting Office in 1990 revealed that the Apache was having alarming maintenance problems, with equipment failing after every 1.5 to 2.4 hours of flight. the GAO report said the Apache "may not be able to operate properly in sustained combat."

The Army's own statistics tended to confirm how serious the problem was. For the first six months of 1990, the AH-64 had a worldwide mission capability of only 71 percent, meaning that 29 percent of all Apaches were out of operation at any given moment. The Army had a mission-capability standard of 75 percent at the time.

The Army and McDonnell Douglas worked hard for more than a year to improve the Apache's performance rating. And they succeeded. Little by little, mission-capability statistics kept edging upward. During the last six months of 1990, the level increased to 77 percent. And during Operation Desert Shield, the AH-64s in the Persian Gulf were mission-capable more than 80 percent of the time.

Army maintenance personnel were able to achieve this high rating despite the terrible conditions with which they were confronted. The sand was the worst problem. As fine as talcum powder, it found its way into virtually every moving part of every helicopter assigned to the Persian Gulf.

Sand sucked into helicopter engines was the biggest worry. "It's going to have an effect," Lieut. Col. Bill Tucker, commander of an Army battalion of Apache helicopters, told the *New York Times*. "You can't put a time or date on it. It wears out moving parts of the engines. The sand collects inside the engine, causes it to get hotter, and therefore it doesn't produce as much power."

The gritty sand also pitted the leading edges of spinning helicopter rotor blades. Maintenance crews solved this problem by applying epoxy tape to the blade edges. But the sand wore through the tape, and it had to be changed after several hours of flying time.

To allied troops, the sand was almost as much an enemy as Iraqi soldiers. M-16 rifles, standard weapons for the infantry, had to be stripped and cleaned daily. Air filters in truck engines had to be changed every day, rather than every 30,000 miles.

The key to keeping helicopters operating, according to one official, was to increase the number of inspections and cleanings. Since the fine sand tended to clog filters and air passages, cleaning usually meant blowing parts clean rather than washing them.

Several helicopter manufacturers reported that maintenance crews with female crew chiefs were often more efficient than those with male crew chiefs. They achieved higher readiness rates with the helicopters they served. "I don't know. Maybe women are just more attuned to cleanliness or maybe they must want to prove they can do the job," an engineering officer for a major manufacturer told *Aviation Week and Space Technology*. "Whatever it is, they seem to be more than holding their own."

Of course, the desert heat was a problem, too. Daytime temperatures sometimes soared to 120° F. Bare metal exposed in the sun reached temperatures in excess of 200° F.

Unless covered with protective canopies, helicopters often became so hot that the crew could not even enter the cabins. One crew's solution was to rig a tentlike structure over an aircraft, using the helicopter's rotor mast as the main pole. The tent sheltered both the helicopter and its maintenance crew.

Apaches were in action every day in Iraq. On one sortie, Apache AH-64s helped to destroy a bunker complex and ended up capturing 500 prisoners. During another raid, 41 Iraqi soldiers fled a bunker waving a white flag after an Apache attack. "They probably never saw one before," one pilot remarked.

The war in the Persian Gulf came to an end following what some observers have called the biggest tank battle since World War II. It took place just west/southwest of Basra, where Iraq's military headquarters was located.

U.S. armored columns raced into the area in an effort to trap Iraqi divisions and keep their tanks and other armored vehicles from escaping northwest to Baghdad. Hundreds of American tanks and helicopters were involved. The fighting lasted for two days.

Iraq lost more than 200 tanks during the battle. The Department of Defense credited one Apache with destroying no less than eight of Iraq's best tanks, Soviet-built T-72s.

In years to come, the Apache may have even more firepower than it does today. Plans have been made for the AH-64 to carry air-to-air weapons, specifically the Stinger missile. The Stinger was chosen be-

The Apache was designed to fly to the battlezone at altitudes measured in tens, rather than thousands, of feet. In this way, the aircraft evades enemy radar and antiaircraft defenses. (McDonnell Douglas Helicopter Company)

cause it is light in weight. It could be carried even on much smaller helicopters, such as the OH-58, a scout aircraft (page 69). A launcher for a pair of Stingers, along with the necessary electronic and sighting systems, weighs only 123 pounds. Fired by Afghan ground forces, the Stinger was highly effective when used against Soviet Hind helicopters in Afghanistan.

Tests have been conducted in which the Apache carried up to four Stingers, which were mounted in pairs on each of the aircraft's stub wings. At the U.S. Army's White Sands, New Mexico range, missile firings were made while the Apache hovered and also during forward flight at around 90 miles an hour. Although the testing began in 1987, it is not likely the Apache will be equipped with Stingers until late in the 1990s.

Nevertheless, the AH-64 is perfectly capable of air-to-air combat. It can bring down a hostile plane with its 30mm chain gun, its rockets or even with a Hellfire missile. In November 1990, the Army conducted tests at the Yuma (Arizona) Proving Grounds in which the Hellfire was used successfully against "enemy" helicopters.

As the decade of the 1990s began, the Army could boast aerial tank-killers of several different types and sizes, such as Sikorsky's UH-60 Black Hawk (page 82). Although classified as a utility helicopter, it was perfectly capable of handling antitank missions if called upon to do so. There was the Hughes 530MG Defender, a day/night all-weather gunship, and the Bell 406 Combat Scout, a reconnaissance aircraft with attack capabilities.

Other combat aircraft included Sikorsky's H-76, a troop transport that could serve as tank-killer. And, of course, there was Bell's AH-1 Cobra (page 30), whose reputation as an antitank weapon dated back to the Vietnam era.

But none of these could really compare with the AH-64 Apache, the ultimate antitank gunship. And tomorrow's Apache, with 21st-century avionics and powerful air-to-air weapons, is sure to be even more of a technological wonder than today's.

2   Mil Mi-24 HIND (RUSSIA)

Originally intended as a transport, the Mi-24 Hind served as the Soviet Union's No. 1 helicopter gunship. (U.S. Navy)

Originally designed as a battlefield helicopter by the Soviet Union, with the primary mission of transporting an eight-man combat team behind enemy lines, the Mi-24 Hind still has that capability. But through the years it has become much more heavily armed than it once was. Now classified as a gunship, it carries a wide range of weapons, including laser-guided homing missiles.

Mi-24D HIND FACT SHEET

Designer: Mil Design Bureau

Type: Armed troop transport

Power Plant: Two Isotov TV-3-117 turboshafts, each delivering 2,200 horsepower

Length: 52 ft., 5 in.

Height: 21 ft., 4 in.

Maximum Takeoff Weight: 24,250 lb.

Main Rotor Diameter: 55 ft., 9 in.

Crew: (2) Pilot and weapons systems operator

First Flight: 1972

Cruising Speed: 185 mph

Range: 280 mi.

As with any troop carrier, the Mi-24 Hind is a large helicopter, with an accent on speed more than on maneuverability. Two short wings provide as much as one-quarter of the aircraft's lift. The wings also serve as launching platforms for the weapons the Hind carries.

The original model, the Mi-24 Hind-A, was flown by units of the Soviet Union's army in East Germany beginning in 1974. Experience there on border patrol missions, as well as research into American helicopter missions in Vietnam, caused the Soviets to make important changes in the aircraft.

The modified Hind is much more of a flying tank. More powerful engines have been installed. The cockpit has been redesigned. The pilot and weapons-systems operator no longer sit side-by-side. In the present-day Hind, the weapons-systems operator is in front, while the pilot is above and behind the gunner. This arrangement provides increased visibility for crew members.

Both crew positions are heavily armored in the new version of the aircraft. A four-barrel 12.7mm Gatling-type machine gun in mounted in the aircraft's nose, giving the Hind the ability to attack other helicopters as well as surface targets. The aircraft still has enough cabin space to be able to deliver an eight-member infantry team to the combat zone.

When on the attack, the Hind uses speed, not stealth, to do its job. It approaches its target from a relatively high altitude, then makes a steep dive while raking the enemy with missile fire. The aircraft is also used to support armored thrusts against enemy tanks.

The Hind may have one serious failing. Unlike the AH-64 Apache (page 00), the Soviet helicopter has not been built to withstand high-G maneuvers. Several Hinds are known to have crashed when their rotor blades sliced into their tail booms during abrupt changes in direction.

The designation "Mi" in Mi-24 is derived from the name of Mikhail L. Mil, who was to Soviet helicopters what Thomas Edison was to the light bulb. Mil became involved in Soviet helicopter research in the early 1930s and remained an important factor in its development until his death in 1970. His Mi-1, the first Soviet helicopter to be mass-produced, was designed in 1949, first flown in 1950, and introduced into active service in 1951.

The nickname "Hind" is not a Soviet term but one applied to the Mi-24 by NATO. In the cold-war years of the 1960s and 1970s, the Soviets seldom revealed any information about their aircraft. They wouldn't even say how their planes were to be designated. To fill the information gap, NATO developed its own system of naming Soviet planes and other aircraft. In each case, the aircraft's nickname was to begin with a letter of its type—"F" for Fighters, "B" for bombers, and "H" for helicopters. Thus, we had such Soviet fighters as the Foxbat, Fulcrum and Flanker, and such bombers as the Blackjack, Bear and Backfire. Helicopters were named Hip, Hook—and Hind.

The initial model of the Hind, the Hind-A, was first flown in 1972. Production models of the aircraft were first seen in service in East Germany during the spring of 1974. In the years since, the aircraft has gone through these modifications:

Mi-24 Hind-A—The first production version, an assault helicopter with a crew of three—pilot, copilot/gunner and engineer.

Mi-24 Hind-B—Similar to the Hind-A, except the auxiliary wings were given a slight downward tilt.

Mi-24 Hind-C—The training version of the aircraft; similar to the Hind-A, but without the nose gun and other armament.

Mi-24 Hind D—Similar to the Hind-A, but with more powerful engines and heavily armored seating for the pilot and gunner. (Other details listed in the Fact Sheet.)

Mi-24 Hind-E—Similar to the Hind-D but with the capability of carrying up to 12 radio-guided, tube-launched antitank missiles. Also, underwing pylons are provided for air-to-air missiles.

Mi-24 Hind-F—Similiar to the Hind-E, but with a twin-barrel 30mm gun mounted on the right side of the fuselage, replacing the nose gun and its turret.

Hi-24 Hind-G—First identified at Chernobyl after the accident at the nuclear power station there in 1986, the Hind-G features "clutching hand" devices, used for picking up radioactive rubble. These extend from wing pylons, instead of wing weapons attachments. Only a small number of Hind-Gs were built.

For years, Soviet manufacturing and assembly plants at Rostov and Arsenyev produced Hinds at the rate of about 15 a month. More than 2,400 Hinds were built, with most going to Soviet army units.

Hind-D and Hind-E helicopters were popular with most Warsaw Pact countries, including Bulgaria, Czechoslovakia, East Germany, Hungary and Poland. These are formerly communist nations of Europe that were bound together in a military alliance under the command of the Soviet Union. They signed the Warsaw Pact in 1955 in the city of Warsaw, Poland, claiming that the merging of their military interests was a response to the creation of the North Atlantic Treaty Organization (NATO), an alliance that had been formed by Canada, the United States and its European allies in 1949. The Warsaw Pact alliance disbanded in 1991.

Aside from the Warsaw Pact nations, there have been many other customers for the Mi-24. Afghanistan, Algeria, Angola, Cuba, India, Iraq, Mozambique, North Korea, North Vietnam and South Yemen have ordered the aircraft.

In 1979, the Soviet Union began what was to become a long and bitter struggle to take over Afghanistan, a land-locked nation in central Asia. Afghanistan shares its northern border with what was then the Soviet Union. Pakistan is to the east and south, Iran to the west.

A group sympathetic to the Soviet Union took control of the government of Afghanistan in 1978. The following year and in 1980, the Soviet Union invaded Afghanistan with thousands of troops and tons of equipment. The Soviet soldiers fanned out to take control of towns and key roads. But the Afghans fought back fiercely. Many thousands of Moslem "holy warriors," or *mujahadin*, organized themselves into guerrilla bands to wage war against the occupation forces.

The fighting lasted for nine years, or until 1988, when United Nations representatives hammered out a cease-fire agreement. Many observers compared the Soviet Union's experience in Afghanistan to that of the United States in Vietnam. (In 1990, Soviet Foreign

Minister Eduard Shevardnadze, looking back, called the Soviet invasion of Afghanistan illegal. He said his nation had "violated the norms of proper behavior.")

During the war, the fast, heavily armored Mi-24 Hind operated when and where it wanted. One tactic was for a single helicopter to draw fire from resistance outposts. Other helicopters following it would then attack the Afghan positions. Helicopters were also used for actual bombardment.

The Afghan guerrillas had no weapons to bring down the Hind-24— at first. The situation changed in 1985. That year, the United States and Great Britain began to supply the Afghan guerrillas with portable, shoulder-launched antiaircraft missiles, specifically, the American Stinger and British blowpipe missiles.

These one-man antiaircraft missiles balanced the scales. By early 1989, when they began withdrawing their forces from Afghanistan, the Soviets had lost close to 1,000 aircraft, 80 percent of which were helicopters. The Mi-24 Hind accounted for more than 200 of those losses.

Soviet helicopter pilots were quick to adopt a number of tactics to make themselves and their aircraft less vulnerable. Flights were scheduled at higher altitudes, and instead of making long, low approaches, they came into the landing zones at high altitudes and then dropped down as fast as possible. They also began firing flares in an effort to provide decoy targets for the infrared-seeking missiles.

To some extent, the tactics were successful. In the final months of the war, losses were less severe then they had been earlier.

One of the Hind's major shortcomings in combat was its size. More than 57 feet long and about 6 1/4 feet wide, it offered a sizable target to antiaircraft batteries or even random gunfire from the ground. The great number of Hinds brought down by one-man guided missiles in Afghanistan is proof of that.

In the early 1980s, when the Soviets began development of a new attack helicopter, they made it smaller and lighter than the Hind. Named the Havoc by NATO, the Mi-28 was planned exclusively as a ground-assault helicopter, not a troop carrier.

Three prototypes of the Mi-28 were built, one of which was displayed at the 1989 Paris Air Show. Like the Mi-24, the Mi-28 had stubby wings with a slight downward slant. But the Havoc's wings were swept back, indicating it might have been faster than the Hind. The Mi-28 was believed to be powered by a pair of Isotov TV3-117 turboshaft engines, the same engines that are common to the Mi-24.

Mi-28 Havoc, characterized by swept-back stub wings, was planned as a successor to the Mi-24 Hind. (Department of Defense)

The Mi-28 is armed with a 30mm gun, the barrel of which juts out from a pod slung beneath the aircraft's nose. Wing pylons give the helicopter the ability to carry 16 antitank missiles, or from four to eight air-to-air missiles.

Military observers expected to see the Mi-28 Havoc on active duty with the Soviet army beginning in 1990 or 1991. But with the political breakup of the Soviet Union in 1991, the future of the Havoc, like the future of the entire nation, is in question.

3   BELL UH-1 IROQUOIS

The UH-1, nicknamed the Huey, is the most widely used helicopter in the world.
(Bell Helicopter Textron)

In the history of military aviation, there are several planes that are recognized for their quality and style. They're classics. They include the P-51 Mustang, the best fighter plane of World War II, and the B-52 Stratofortress, the nation's first intercontinental strategic bomber. Introduced in 1954, the B-52 was an important factor in the Persian Gulf War in 1991 and is still in service today.

UH-1H IROQUOIS FACT SHEET

Manufacturer: Bell Helicopter Textron

Type: General purpose helicopter

Power Plant: One Lycoming T53-L-13 turboshaft, delivering 1,400 horsepower

Length: 57 ft., 10 in.

Height: 11 ft., 10 in.

Maximum Takeoff Weight: 9,500 lb.

Main Rotor Diameter: 48 ft., 3 in.

Crew: (2) Pilot, copilot

First Flight: 1961

Cruising Speed: 135 mph

Range: 280 mi.

When it comes to helicopters, there is really only one that deserves classic status. It is Bell Aircraft's UH-1 Iroquois, better known as the Huey (after its original military designation, HU-1).

Introduced in Vietnam in 1962, the Huey now ranks as the most widely used helicopter in the world. More than 9,000 Hueys have been produced, and the helicopter is flown in 40 countries.

A single-engine, single-rotor aircraft, the Huey was the workhorse of the Vietnam War. Indeed, the Huey and its distinctive "tadpole" shape became the very symbol of that war.

While the Huey was used for troop transport, armed patrol and escort in Vietnam, its most impressive role was as a medical evacuation helicopter. At the peak of the fighting in Vietnam, every infantry division had a medical battalion, and most of these battalions were equipped with helicopter ambulances.

The chief task of the "medevac" helicopter was to fly wounded soldiers to a medical clearing station. From there, other helicopters moved the patients to field hospitals.

In some battlefield situations, it was not possible for the Huey to land. While the aircraft hovered, the crew lowered a hoist to haul the wounded

soldier aboard. Of course, the helicopter made an inviting target for enemy fire while it hovered. While dozens of Hueys were hit, many thousands of casualties were rescued in this way. In fact, by the end of the war, more than 370,000 casualties had been moved by helicopters.

Today's Army Huey, designated the UH-1H, is still used for casualty evacuation, as well as for resupply missions, and as a command and control aircraft. The Army's Huey fleet numbers some 2,721 aircraft.

A word about the Huey's rotor system. In the earliest versions of the aircraft, the blades were made of long strips of aluminum, which were laminated together. But over the years, these were replaced by much stronger blades made of a fiberglass composite molded over a honeycombed core.

The leading edge of the blade is sheathed on a thin layer of stainless steel. This enables the blade to slice through small tree branches or other obstructions that helicopters sometimes encounter when flying at low levels.

The Huey's fuselage is similar to that of a sleek racing car in that it is of monocoque construction—a composite skin over a lightweight metal frame. This construction system enables the skin to absorb much of the stress to which the aircraft is subjected.

The pilot sits in the left-hand seat, the copilot in the right. When the Huey is assigned a troop carrier or gunship mission, a third crew member serves as a gunner. When the aircraft is fitted out as a flying ambulance, a medic travels in the main compartment.

Avionics equipment carried by the UH-1H includes UHF, FM and VHF radios, a friend-or-foe identification system and sophisticated navigation aids. When they're needed, the aircraft can be fitted out with a rescue hoist, cargo hook and additional fuel tanks.

Through the years, Hueys have been armed with just about every type of weapon suitable for a helicopter of its particular weight and speed. But several types of armament have come to be regarded as standard. These include four 7.62mm machine guns, two mounted on each side of the aircraft. These are fed from ammunition trays stored on the cabin floor, each tray holding 6,600 rounds.

In addition, the Huey normally carries 2.75-inch free-flight rockets, packaged in containers of various sizes. For example, a 48-shot rocket system was used in Vietnam in 1963.

The Huey is also equipped with a 40mm grenade launcher. Known as the "Thumper" or "Chunker" for the distinctive sound it makes, the weapon can fire 220 to 240 shots per minute at a range of one mile.

The Huey can also carry 20mm or 25mm cannons in pod mounts, 50-caliber machine guns, various kinds of antitank guided missiles, and, when serving with naval forces, depth charges or torpedoes.

The story of the Huey goes back to 1954, the year the U.S. Army called for a design competition for a new helicopter that would be able to carry an 800-pound payload on a round-trip of 200 nautical miles (227 "land" miles) at a cruising speed of 100 knots (114 miles per hour). The Army planned to use the aircraft to carry troops, supplies and equipment, and also to transport wounded soldiers from the battlefield.

The helicopter's value as a flying ambulance had been clearly proven time and again during the Korean War, which had ended in 1953. Medevac helicopters, as they were called, were often assigned to pick up wounded soldiers on the battlefield where they had fallen, and then whisk them directly to a field hospital. The bravery of the helicopter pilots and their rescue crews, who often undertook their missions in the midst of enemy fire, was documented in countless books and movies, and on the "M*A*S*H" television series, which is still being rerun. (M*A*S*H stands for Mobile Army Surgical Hospital.) While medical-evacuation helicopters of the 1950s carried only one wounded soldier at a time, they saved many hundreds of lives.

The first battlefield helicopters had other failings besides their lack of size. Breakdowns were frequent. A helicopter required many hours of maintenance just to be able to fly for an hour or so.

The Army looked forward to overcoming this problem by having the new helicopter equipped with a gas-turbine engine. Such an engine would be more reliable and easier to maintain than the piston engines that had powered earlier helicopters. The gas-turbine engine would also be more powerful.

In the mid-1950s, jet engines were being used in most of the world's bombers and fighter planes. These were jet engines of the simplest type—turbojets. They pushed a jet of air backward with much more force and speed than the propeller engine.

The turboshaft engine, an offshoot of the pure jet, was thought to be the logical choice for the helicopter. (Both the turboshaft and the turbojet are gas turbines.) In the turboshaft engine, the high velocity gases are used to drive a power turbine. The turbine, in turn, drives the rotor shaft that turns the propeller blades.

The turboshaft has countless advantages over the piston engine. It is less complex and has fewer parts, making it easier to maintain. It is lighter in weight, an advantage that makes for an increased payload. It is easier to start and doesn't have to be warmed up before flight. And since the turboshaft engine is smaller in size, it can be mounted on top of the helicopter, which makes for more cabin space. Piston engines were installed inside the fuselage.

Some 20 helicopter companies entered the Army's design competition. Bell Helicopter of Fort Worth, Texas, was the winner (now known as Bell Helicopter Textron). In June 1955, Bell was awarded a contract to build three prototypes, which were to be designated XH-40s.

The first of the XH-40s made its first flight in October 1956. As the aircraft left the ground, its spinning rotor filled the air with a loud *whop - whop - whop*, sound that already had come to be identified with helicopters. But the aircraft also gave off a high-pitched whine from its gas-turbine engine, which was to become as familiar as the thump of the rotor blade.

Shortly after the first flight of the XH-40, the Army ordered six more prototypes. These, like the first three, were extensively tested. Some were flown in the desert heat of Edwards Air Force Base near Rosamond, California. Others were tested in the extreme cold of Alaska.

There were few problems with the new aircraft. Even before testing was completed, the Army ordered the first production models.

The Army, which has a policy of naming helicopters after Indian tribes, named the new aircraft the HU-1A Iroquois. But most soldiers turned the helicopter's HU designation into a nickname—"Huey." So widely accepted did the name become, that Bell eventually stamped HUEY on the helicopter's right control panel. (The left pedal was stamped with the word BELL.)

In 1962, when the Department of Defense announced a uniform aircraft designation system for the Army, Navy, Air Force and Marine Corps (page 000), the HU-1 Iroquois became the UH-1 Iroquois. But most people still called it the Huey.

The XH-40 prototypes had a single turboshaft engine that produced 700 horsepower. The aircraft could carry a total load, including fuel, of 5,800 pounds. Of this, some 2,200 pounds could be represented by the crew, passengers and payload. The aircraft could cruise at 125 miles per hour and had a top speed of close to 140 mph. Its maximum range was 290 miles.

The HU-1A (or UH-1A) was much the same as the XH-40, except that it was powered with an 806-horsepower Lycoming engine. This increased the aircraft's cruising speed to about 130 mph, its top speed to almost 150 mph, and its range to 380 miles.

At the same time the Huey was being developed, an ongoing war in Southeast Asia was growing into an international conflict. Vietnam, a small country in Southeast Asia about the size of New Mexico, was divided into communist-ruled North Vietnam and noncommunist South Vietnam. North Vietnamese and communist-trained South Vietnamese rebels, known as Viet Cong, fought to gain control of South Vietnam. The United States and the South Vietnamese Army tried to prevent the takeover, but failed.

The war began in 1957 and lasted until 1975. It was the longest war in which the United States has ever been involved.

The helicopter's role as a battlefield weapon was forever shaped by the war in Vietnam. Thousands of helicopters of many different types saw duty there. Indeed, it has been called the "Helicopter War."

Besides the Bell UH-1 (the Huey) used chiefly for medical evacuation and troop transport, Vietnam helicopters included Sikorsky's CH-53, a heavy lifter; Bell's OH-58, a patrol aircraft; Hughes's OH-6, used for reconnaissance; and Sikorsky's HH-3, which played a heroic role in search and rescue.

Before these aircraft became available to American and South Vietnamese forces in Vietnam, the Army depended to a large degree on CH-21 Shawnee transport helicopters built by Piasecki Aircraft. In service with the Army since 1954, the CH-21 could carry 15 soldiers, but had a top speed of only 75 miles an hour, which made the aircraft an easy target for enemy ground fire.

Just before Christmas in 1962, South Vietnamese forces planned to launch an attack near Tuy Hoa, with the troops to be ferried to the battle zone aboard 29 CH-21s. The first three helicopters landed safely, but six others were hit by enemy ground fire, causing heavy casualties. An Army spokesperson said the casualties were caused because the landing zone had not been "softened up" before the helicopters went in.

The Army responded by arming the CH-21s with 30-caliber machine guns, which were mounted in the aircraft's doorway. This only partially solved the problem, however, because the gunners could fire

In Vietnam, the Huey played a vital role as the Army's medical evacuation helicopter. (Bell Helicopter Textron)

only from the doorway-side of the aircraft. The other side was still unprotected.

A better solution was to provide the CH-21 and other helicopter transports with armed escort helicopters. UH-1As were among the first aircraft to serve in this role.

Shortly after their arrival in Vietnam, 15 new UH-1As were fitted out with two 2.75-inch rocket pods, each with eight launching tubes. One pod was mounted on each of the helicopter's skids.

A forward-firing machine gun was also mounted on each skid. To protect the helicopter at the sides and rear, gunners with hand-held automatic weapons were posted in the doorways.

A typical combat mission, or "Eagle Flight," as it was called, consisted of four CH-21s carrying South Vietnamese troops and three armed UH-1As providing armed escort. A fourth Huey served as an observer aircraft, commanding and controlling the mission.

The observer's job was to spot an enemy force and then pinpoint a landing zone for the transports. The armed escorts not only provided a blanket of protection, they also played a role as reconnaissance aircraft.

A small single-wing, single-engine, fixed-wing aircraft, the T-28 Trojan, was also assigned to these early missions. Like the Hueys, the T-28s provided close air support.

Sometimes two T-28s would be called upon. One of the aircraft would fly low "S" turns ahead of the helicopter pack, searching for enemy activity and attempting to draw fire away from the helicopters. The other T-28 would fly high "S" turns behind the formation.

The armed helicopter escort of troop-carrying helicopters proved highly successful from the very beginning. Even though the "Eagle Flights" meant there were more helicopters in the air, the number hit by ground fire fell dramatically.

In June 1959, at about the same time the first HU-1As were being delivered, the Army called upon Bell Aircraft to produce a more powerful version of the Iroquois. This aircraft, with a 960-hp Lycoming engine, was designated the HU-1B. It made its first flight in April 1960.

The first UH-1Bs arrived in Vietnam in November 1962. Because their more powerful engine enabled them to carry a bigger payload, the new Hueys could be fitted out with many more weapons. They were also less sensitive to the high humidity and other flying conditions of Vietnam. UH-1Bs became the first helicopter "gunships."

Each UH-1B carried four M-60 7.62mm machine guns, two of which were mounted on each side behind the cargo doors. They could be operated by the pilot and copilot as well as the gunner. The gun turrets had racks for rocket pods and grenade launchers.

As more UH-1Bs arrived in Vietnam, they were used as troop transports, replacing the aging CH-21 Shawnees. When transporting fully equipped troops, the Hueys were not able to carry their normal armament. Their weapons had to be reduced to door-mounted machine guns.

With the retirement of the CH-21s, Eagle Flights were made up exclusively of Hueys. One UH-1B would serve as an aerial command post. Five fully armed Hueys could provide escort for as many as seven Huey troop carriers. A 13th helicopter went along to provide medical evacuation, if necessary.

On a typical mission, the gunships would arrive at the trouble spot first, pinpointing the enemy troops while firing weapons. Once a landing site had been agreed upon, the troopships would land. As the troops were being unloaded, the gunships would continue to pound enemy positions. After unloading, the transports would head back to their base while the gunships again provided cover.

But all-Huey Eagle Flights presented a problem. When a UH-1B was fully loaded with its armament, ammunition and three-person crew, it became a less maneuverable aircraft. It lost some speed, too. As a result, Huey gunships could not keep up with troop-carrying Hueys.

The UH-1C helped to solve the problem. Thanks to a more powerful engine—an 1100-hp Lycoming—and a rotor blade that was wider by several inches, the new aircraft was much faster and a great deal more maneuverable than the earlier Hueys. The UH-1C also had greater range. It could make a round trip of 296 miles, compared to 260 miles for the UH-1B.

The UH-1C was equipped with machine guns and rocket launchers on either side, plus a grenade launcher in the nose. The aircraft carried a crew of four: a pilot, copilot and two gunners. On a gun run, all crewmembers fired weapons. The pilot controlled the rocket launchers, the copilot aimed and fired the grenade launcher, while each of the gunners manned a machine gun.

Some UH-1Cs were upgraded by replacing their 1100-hp Lycomings with engines rated at 1400-hp, also made by Lycoming. This change boosted the Huey's speed, range and rate of climb. The new Hueys were designated UH-1Ms.

In 1971, the enemy in Vietnam stepped up operations by introducing tanks. At first, American and South Vietnamese forces sought to cope with enemy armor with UH-1C and UH-1M gunships. They were armed with rockets, cannons and grenade launchers. While these weapons were somewhat effective, it was apparent that something more powerful was needed.

Before the end of 1971, two UH-1Bs were sent to Vietnam armed with TOW (for tube-launched, optically guided, tracked, wire-guided) missiles. Within two months, the TOW-equipped Hueys had put 26 enemy tanks out of operation, an impressive record. In time, TOW missiles came to rank as one of the Army's most successful anti-armor weapons.

The helicopter gunner practically flies the TOW to its target. Once the missile has been launched, the gunner keeps his eyepiece on the target. By doing so, he enables a small computer aboard the helicopter to track a tiny red light in the missile's tail. The computer compares the location of the missile in flight with the location of the target and automatically figures any course corrections.

Signals to steer the TOW are sent to the missile through two very thin wires that unreel from the missile as it speeds toward the target. The TOW has a range of more than two miles.

When serving as troop transports, the earliest Hueys—the A, B and C models—could carry eight soldiers. But the Army wanted the aircraft to be able to transport a bigger load. In response, Bell developed the UH-1D. Although powered by the same engine used in the UH-1C, the new aircraft was 3 1/2 feet longer than any previous Huey. The increased length enable the UH-1D to carry as many as 12 soldiers into battle. And the aircraft was fitted with two large sliding doors that made loading and unloading much easier.

UH-1Ds started arriving in Vietnam late in 1963. Besides serving as assault transports, UH-1Ds were assigned command-and-control missions. They also served as reconnaissance aircraft and were used for transporting supplies and equipment as well. And, of course, they handled medical evacuation missions. In a medevac role, the UH-1D could carry six litter patients.

Many UH-1Ds were upgraded by being fitted out with a more powerful engine, the 1400-hp Lycoming. These aircraft were designated UH-1D/Hs.

The UH-1D and UH-1H were real workhorses in Vietnam. Nearly 8,000 were built, of which some 5,435 were H models.

The Marine Corps and Navy also flew Hueys in Vietnam. The Marines used the UH-1E, which was similar in design to the Army's UH-1B, as a gunship.

The U.S. Air Force uses UH-1 as a search-and-rescue aircraft. This is the UH-1F. (Bell Helicopter Textron)

But one important difference in the two aircraft was that the Marine Corps' Huey had a rotor brake. On the flight deck of a ship, it was extremely hazardous to allow the rotor blade to gradually spin to a stop. The brake enabled the pilot to stop the blade immediately.

Besides their gunship role, Marine Hueys were used in transporting troops to and from battle for reconnaissance and on observation missions. There were also Marine medical Hueys.

Marine medical missions were often conducted at night in the face of heavy ground fire. The pickup zone would first be illuminated by flare aircraft. Then helicopter gunships would move in, and attempt to smother the enemy guns. Last, the medical Huey would make the pickup.

The Navy turned to Hueys in 1966, not long after being assigned to patrol the vast Mekong Delta of South Vietnam. Crisscrossed by rivers, streams, canals and dikes, the Mekong Delta ranked as one of the world's most productive rice-growing regions. While it made up only about 20 percent of the land area of South Vietnam, some 60 percent of the population lived there.

The region was being overrun with Viet Cong at the time the Navy was handed the responsibility of gaining control of the delta waterways and restraining enemy movement. To do the job, the Navy relied upon fast river-patrol boats, which were supported by UH-1B gunships. At first, the Navy's helicopters were flown by Army crews. But by the fall of 1967, the Navy was doing its own flying.

Navy helicopter crews operating in the Mekong Delta came to be known as Seawolves. They were on alert 24 hours a day. It took no longer than three minutes to get a crew into the air. On a typical mission, two helicopters answered the call. While one attacked the target, which could be a sampan, a bunker or fleeing troops, the other Huey provided cover.

The U.S. Air Force was the fourth branch of the armed forces to operate Hueys in Vietnam. The Air Force used UH-1Fs chiefly on search-and-rescue missions.

In 1970, the Air Force ordered 30 Hueys. While they were intended mainly for search and rescue, they were also to be used for transporting support crews at missile sites. Designated HH-1Hs, these aircraft are still on active duty with the Air Force.

While the Huey served gallantly in Vietnam, it suffered terrible losses. It lacked heavy weapons for self-defense. It had no armored cockpit for the crew. As a result, the aircraft was vulnerable to enemy groundfire at low altitudes. Even a few well placed shots could bring it down. More than 5,000 Hueys were lost during the war.

In the decades since Vietnam, the UH-1 has continued to serve with the Army, Navy, Marine Corps and Air Force. Of course, today's Hueys, with their space-age composites and state-of-the-art electronics, are a far cry from those UH-1As, Bs, Cs, Ds and Hs that saved so many lives during the Vietnam War years.

4   BELL AH-1 COBRA

The first clash of arms in the Persian Gulf War, with the first American unit to engage troops in face-to-face combat, took place shortly after midnight on the last Wednesday in January 1991. The call came in—a "strip alert," the Marines call it—to the 369th Marine Light Attack Squadron based in Saudi Arabia near the border of Kuwait, saying that 25 Iraqi vehicles had crossed the border and were headed south.

Within minutes, the squadron's four AH-1W SuperCobras were in the air. The stubby wings of each aircraft were crammed with rockets to destroy enemy tanks and other armored vehicles, and the flares to locate them.

AH-1W SUPERCOBRA FACT SHEET

Manufacturer: Bell Helicopter Textron

Type: Light attack helicopter

Power Plant: Two General Electric T700-GE-401 turboshafts, each delivering 1,690 horsepower

Length: 45 ft., 6 in.

Height: 14 ft., 2 in.

Maximum Takeoff Weight: 14,750 lb.

Main Rotor Diameter: 48 ft.

Crew: (2) Pilot, copilot

First Flight: 1980

Cruising Speed: 175 mph

Range: 395 mi.

Keeping close to the desert floor, the pilots nosed their short, slim-bodied aircraft toward a dusty roadway about a mile north of the center of Khafji, a coastal city only about 10 miles south of the Kuwait border. There they discovered a convoy of six Iraqi troop carriers, the size of large trucks. The vehicles were parked, the small cannons in their roof turrets silent.

The SuperCobras attacked. One rocket after another slammed into the troop carriers.

Three of the troop carriers started their engines and tried to flee. But the other three stayed to fight, each firing at least one round at the swarming helicopters. The SuperCobras immediately unleashed another salvo of rockets, destroying two of the troop carriers. The third appeared to get away.

Later, back at their base, Major Michael Steele, one of the Marine pilots, said that the Iraqis had lived up to their reputation to fight even when overmatched. "I expected some of them to fight, and they did," he said. Major Steele and many other frontline troops believed the Iraqi troops would put up a stiff fight once the ground war began. They believed the land war would go on for months, not weeks.

The AH-1W SuperCobra has earned a reputation as a "do anything, go anywhere" helicopter. (Bell Aircraft Textron)

Fortunately, they were wrong. On February 24, 1991, allied forces launched a massive ground assault against Iraq. Just four days later, Iraq agreed to peace terms, and President George Bush could announce, "Kuwait is liberated. Iraq's army is defeated. Our military objectives are met."

A devastating series of air attacks, which had begun on January 17, 1991, had paved the way for the allied victory. According to one estimate, Iraq was hit with more than 40,000 sorties. The AH-1W SuperCobra was only one of a tremendous variety of aircraft that had pounded Iraq.

While the SuperCobra, the latest in a long line of Cobras that stretches back to the 1960s, is perfectly capable of attacking enemy armor, as it did in Iraq, that is not its primary mission. The helicopter was developed to serve as an escort aircraft for troop-carrying helicopters. It also can be used to provide close-in fire support, pinpoint targets for artillery or other helicopters, and perform reconnaissance duties.

As that run-down may suggest, the SuperCobra is a "do anything, go anywhere" helicopter. First flown in Vietnam in 1967, it has gone through several upgradings. Today's version is faster, more powerful, and has far greater range than earlier models. To the Marine Corps, it's a "lean, mean, fighting machine."

The SuperCobra is equipped with a great array of weapons. These include rockets, a 20mm cannon, and air-to-ground missiles. It has what is called "dual antiarmor capability." This means that it can be equipped to fire either the TOW or laser-guided Hellfire missiles. It is the only attack helicopter with this capability.

The SuperCobra is also capable of carrying two Sidewinder missiles. These are heat-seeking missiles; they have the ability to literally fly up the white-hot tailpipe of an enemy aircraft. They enable the SuperCobra to take on an enemy helicopter or even a fighter in a direct nose-to-nose scrap.

The Sidewinder was the first successful air-to-air missile and also the first infrared weapon to be used by United States forces. The newest version of the weapon has what is known as an "off boresight" capability. This means that the aircraft firing the missile doesn't necessarily have to be facing its target at the moment of firing, yet the missile will still get there.

Air-to-air combat is part of the Cobra's history, incidentally. During the 1982 war between Israel and Lebanon, an Israeli Air Force AH-1S Cobra, another advanced version of the aircraft, destroyed a Syrian Gazelle antitank helicopter, blasting it with a TOW missile. Military experts believe that such air-to-air encounters are likely to occur more frequently in any future conflicts.

The Cobra was developed in the mid-1960s, a period when the war in Vietnam was getting hotter in terms of both manpower and firepower. The Army's most heavily armed helicopter gunship at the time was the UH-1B Huey.

But the Huey wasn't a "true" gunship. It was merely a utility helicopter in which guns and other weapons had been installed. It was limited in speed, range and the size of its payload. What the Army wanted was a helicopter that was designed from the ground up as a gunship.

In response to the Army's wishes, Bell Aircraft redesigned the Huey to produce an aircraft with a narrower airframe (which made for a smaller target), a more powerful engine and tandem seating. In the Huey, the crewmembers sat side-by-side. The pilot now sat above and behind the copilot/gunner. Both had excellent visibility through the bubble cockpit.

The new aircraft was given the designation UH-1H. But in a short time this was changed to AH-1G. The UH-1H designation was assigned to a new model of the troop-carrying Huey.

At the time, the nickname Cobra was being used for all gunships in Vietnam. When the AH-1G arrived upon the scene, it was officially called the HueyCobra. It thus became the only Army helicopter <u>not</u> to be named after an Indian tribe.

The HueyCobra first flew in September 1965. Surely one reason for the success it was to enjoy was its simplicity. Like its predecessor, the Huey, the Cobra was a single-rotor aircraft. This is the easiest type of helicopter to fly.

A single-rotor helicopter has one main rotor mounted above its fuselage. This is, in effect, a rotating wing. While the fixed wing of an airplane provides lift as the craft moves forward, the rotating blades of a helicopter provide lift as they spin.

The whirling rotor blade also produces a turning or twisting force called torque. If the torque were not neutralized, it would tend to spin the fuselage of the helicopter in a direction opposite to that of the rotor. This is a law of physics, expressed by Sir Isaac Newton's Third Law of Motion, which states, "To every action, there is an equal and opposite reaction."

The solution to the problem is a second rotor, a tail rotor, which is mounted vertically on either side of the tail and thus spins at right angles to the main rotor. By generating horizontal thrust, the tail rotor over-comes the tendency of the helicopter to spin in a direction opposite to that of the main rotor. The tail rotor counterbalances the torque. Sometimes called an "anti-torque" rotor, the tail rotor is used in controlling the helicopter's direction (see below).

In piloting a single-rotor helicopter (so called in spite of the second rotor mounted at the tail), such as the UH-1 Iroquois, the pilot operates three basic controls: collective-pitch lever, a control column, and rudder pedals.

The pilot's left hand controls the collective-pitch lever. By moving the lever up or down, the pilot changes the pitch of the rotor blades.

When the pilot raises the lever, blade pitch is increased. This also increases the lift generated by the spinning blades. When the lifting force becomes greater than the pull of gravity, the helicopter goes straight up.

Lowering the collective-pitch lever decreases the pitch and reduces the amount of lift. The helicopter descends.

To hover, the pilot decreases the pitch just enough to counteract the pull of gravity. The helicopter then maintains a constant altitude.

At the same time that the pilot's left hand is operating the collective-pitch lever, the right hand operates the control column, which is a stick at the pilot's right hand or between the pilot's knees. The control stick can be tilted in any direction. The helicopter moves in whatever direction the pilot tilts it.

Suppose the pilot wants to move the helicopter forward. The pilot tilts the control column forward. This causes the pitch of the rotor blades to be greatest just before they pass over the tail. The blades have the least pitch just before they reach the nose. The result is that the rotor tilts upward in the rear and the helicopter flies forward. Tilting the control column back has the opposite effect.

The pilot uses the rudder pedals to turn. The rudders control the pitch of the tail rotor blades.

Suppose the pilot wishes to swing the helicopter to the left. The pilot steps on the left rudder pedal. This increases the pitch of the tail-rotor blades, which pushes the tail in a direction opposite to the torque's pressure. The tail swings to the right and the helicopter's nose goes to the left.

To turn to the right, the pilot presses down on the right rudder pedal, decreasing the pitch. The torque then swings the tail to the left—and the nose to the right.

As this may suggest, flying a helicopter is a delicate piece of business. Pilots who have flown both types of aircraft say it is harder to fly a helicopter than a fixed-wing aircraft, that is, an airplane.

The helicopter pilot frequently must be concerned with more than one set of controls at the same time, trying to keep them in balance. The difficulty is increased in the case of the military pilot, who, when in battle, often seeks to survive by avoiding detection. This means keeping low, flying only a few yards from the ground or just above the tree tops. The pilot uses clumps of trees, small hills, and rock formations to keep concealed.

This is called nap-of-the-earth (NOE) flying. It is very demanding, requiring enormous skill on the part of the pilot. There is no margin for error.

Besides having to fly the aircraft, the Cobra pilot was also responsible for launching the wing-mounted weapons. The copilot/gunner controlled a chin turret that housed a 20mm or 30mm cannon. The copilot/gunner was also in charge of the sighting system in the nose.

The nose-mounted sight was singled out as one of the weaknesses of the HueyCobra. What would have been better was a roof-mounted sight. When the sighting system is in the helicopter's nose, it forces the pilot to expose the aircraft completely when tracking and aiming the wire-guided TOW missile and other weapons. The pilot cannot maintain a low, hull-down position. The helicopter is thus easier to detect and becomes a fat target for enemy ground fire.

Despite this failing, the Army was very enthusiastic about the HueyCobra. Since it was to be manufactured by Bell and was based upon the Huey, they were assured it wouldn't be long before it was rolling off the assembly line. No long period of testing would be necessary. The normal glitches encountered in the development of a new aircraft would be few.

And since the HueyCobra was so similar to the Huey, maintenance would be easier. The HueyCobra used many of the same parts as the Huey. Mechanics and electronics technicians would be able to service the HueyCobra with little or no retraining.

These weren't the only benefits. Powered by a 1400-horsepower Lycoming engine, the AH-16 had a maximum cruising speed of more than 170 miles an hour. It could top 200 mph in a shallow dive. Such statistics meant the HueyCobra would have no trouble flying escort for even the latest-model troop-carrying transports.

Like the Huey, the HueyCobra had a skid-type landing system. One important new feature was the HueyCobra's stub wings. At high speeds, the wings provided additional lift, which meant the pilot didn't have to rely quite so much on the main rotor. This improved

An Army AH-1 Huey-Cobra prepares to touch down on the flight deck of the amphibious assault ship Iwo Jima *during landing drills.* (Department of Defense)

the handling qualities of the new aircraft. Some pilots said that flying a HueyCobra was something like flying a fixed-wing aircraft.

The wings provided one other important benefit. They could be used to carry some of the HueyCobra's great array of weapons.

These included a turret-mounted 7.62mm minigun, a fierce multiple-barrel weapon. The minigun system was based upon that of the Civil War Gatling gun, an early type of machine gun that featured a revolving cluster of barrels. During every turn of the cluster, each barrel automatically loaded and fired. The newly designed version of the gun has six barrels and can fire as many as 3,000 rounds per minute.

Tested on UH-1Bs in Vietnam, the first miniguns to be used operationally were mounted on Huey-Cobras in 1966. There was no better weapon for covering a landing zone.

The gunner could move the minigun turret up or down or to the left or right. The pilot could also fire the gun, but when fired by the pilot, the gun had to be locked in a forward-firing position. Essentially, the pilot aimed the gun by aiming the aircraft itself.

The front-turret minigun was later replaced by two side pods, each enclosing a pair of miniguns. These boosted the rate of fire to 4,400 rounds per minute.

The 40mm grenade launcher was another weapon used by the Huey-Cobra. It fulfilled the need for a large-caliber weapon with a rapid rate of fire—240 shots per minute. The grenade launcher enabled a pilot to lay down a frightful barrage of high explosives in clearing a landing zone.

Many different combinations of other weapons could be carried beneath the HueyCobra's stubby wings. These included six-barreled 20mm cannons, and rocket pods holding as many as 19 2.75-inch Folding Fin Aerial Rockets.

Although the HueyCobra depended on speed, agility and its relatively small profile for survival in conflict, the aircraft was fitted with armor plating in several key areas. Armor protected crew members on each side. (For protection from gunfire from the front, each crew member wore an armored vest.) Engine parts were also protected by armor. The HueyCobra's fuel tank was self-sealing. Many of the helicopter's vital parts were designed to absorb a hit from a .30-caliber bullet and survive.

The first HueyCobras were delivered to the U.S. Army in Vietnam late in 1967. On September 4 that year, the aircraft was credited with its first kill—a small Viet Cong boat, or *sampan*, in the Mekong Delta.

In the months that followed, HueyCobra gunships demonstrated their great value in many different ways. Time after time, they used their guns and rockets to pound enemy forces, allowing pinned-down American and South Vietnamese troops to escape. In addition, they provided protection for troop-carrying helicopters. To the Viet Cong, the Huey-Cobra became known as "Whispering Death."

HueyCobras were also used to locate targets and direct fire for artillery and air strikes. After the fireworks, the AH-1G played a reconnaissance role, returning to appraise the damage.

While HueyCobras normally flew at around 1,500 feet, the aircraft's guns were accurate at altitudes of up to 4,000 feet. The aircraft could operate when the weather turned bad and low ceilings prevented Air Force and Navy close-support aircraft from flying.

When the Viet Cong began using Soviet-made SAM (surface-to-air) heat-seeking missiles as antiaircraft weapons, it was a sad day for the Army's fleet of HueyCobras. The missiles, which homed in on a helicopter's hot exhaust, represented a deadly threat on almost every mission.

But the Army managed to come up with a clever answer to the problem. It took the form of a metal shield that deflected the engine's hot exhaust into the great rush of air generated by the rotor blade. The result was the

The Marine Corps flies both the AH-1J SeaCobra and AH-1W SuperCobra (above).
(Bell Aircraft Textron)

same as blowing a puff of smoke into an electric fan. The exhaust fumes were dispersed in every direction, and no longer were the SAMs able to use them for guidance. While the shield added more weight to the HueyCobra, it sharply reduced the SAM menace.

In the years following the Vietnam War, several other versions of the Cobra were produced. There was the AH-1Q, the Army's TOW-carrying tank-killer, called the KingCobra.

Powered by a 2,850-horsepower Lycoming, the AH-1Q had greater fuel capacity than earlier versions of the aircraft, and a wingspan of 13 feet—two feet more than the wingspan of the AH-1G. This additional length provided more space for mounting rockets and other weapons.

The biggest advance, however, had to do with electronics. The King-Cobra had night vision, thanks to Low Light-Level Television (LLLTV) and Forward-Looking Infrared (FLIR) sensors. The KingCobra's nose was lengthened to provide space to stow the new equipment.

The KingCobra made its first flight in 1972. But before very many AH-1Qs were produced, the Army decided that what it really needed was an even more powerful tank buster, one that could carry a greater number of TOW missiles, had better survival qualities, and would be able to operate in virtually any type of environment, from desert heat to Arctic cold. The result was the AH-1S, the first production models of which were delivered to the Army in 1977.

The AH-1J SeaCobra is yet another version of the aircraft. A twin-engine helicopter capable of land- or sea-based operations, the SeaCobra was designed and built for the Marine Corps.

The most recent version is the AH-1W SuperCobra, a star performer in the war in the Persian Gulf. The SuperCobra flew for the first time in 1980. Like the SeaCobra, the SuperCobra is a two-engine aircraft.

By the early 1990s, close to 2,000 HueyCobras, SeaCobras and SuperCobras were in service with the Army, Navy and Marine Corps, and many more were on order.

In the SuperCobra, the pilot sits above and behind the copilot/gunner. Both have excellent visibility.
(Bell Aircraft Textron)

5 AEROSPATIALE AS-366 DAUPHIN (FRANCE)

A French aerospace company, Aerospatiale, has developed one of the most successful helicopter designs of recent years. It's the AS-366 Dauphin 2, a medium-sized, single-rotor transport aircraft that has won worldwide praise for its performance and its multiple uses.

As a combat helicopter, the Dauphin (the word is French for dolphin) can be used for troop transport, search and rescue, medical evacuation, and even as an attack helicopter. Ordered by the Saudi Arabian Air

The U.S. Coast Guard calls the AS-366 the Dolphin and uses the aircraft in search-and-rescue operations. (Aerospatiale)

40

Force, it is used as an anti-ship helicopter, protecting Saudi interests in the Persian Gulf.

The Dauphin is also flown by the U.S. Coast Guard. Known by the Coast Guard as the HH65A Dolphin, the aircraft is used for search-and-rescue missions from ship or shore. It is also sometimes used to help combat drug smuggling.

The Coast Guard Dolphin is equipped with advanced communications, navigation and all-weather search equipment. This includes a nose-mounted "See Hawk" forward-looking infrared sensor to aid in rescue operations at night or in bad weather.

The aircraft's radar is housed in a bulbous radome beneath the helicopter's nose. It has the ability to scan a full 360 degrees.

The first Dolphins were delivered to the Coast Guard in 1984, and by the next year the aircraft was in service at Coast Guard bases and aboard cutters and ice breakers. By 1991, the Coast Guard had taken delivery of 99 Dolphins.

One of the most distinctive features of the AS-366 is its tail rotor. Its 11 blades spin inside a circular housing at the base of the helicopter's tail

The Coast Guard's 99 Dolphins are flown from both ship and shore bases. Scene below is of Floyd Bennett Field in New York City. (George Sullivan)

Dauphin's tail rotor is enclosed within a circular housing beneath the tail fin. Design makes for improved stability and control.
(George Sullivan)

fin. "This design streamlines the aircraft," says Lt. Amy Ezell, a Coast Guard helicopter pilot. "It improves stability and control. It helps make the Dolphin very smooth to fly."

"And when the aircraft is on the ground, it's a safety factor. The ordinary tail rotor, when it's spinning, is like a buzz saw. It's a real hazard for crew members or anyone working around the aircraft."

The four main rotor blades of the Dolphin are made of composite materials. They're exceptionally light in weight, thanks to a honeycomb filling made of fiberglass. The blades attach to a molded glass-and-fiber rotor hub that has a "quick disconnect" system for easy replacement and maintenance.

The Dauphin has a standard crew of two, a pilot and copilot. With the Coast Guard, a third crew member is often added as a hoist operator. The aircraft can carry as many as 14 passengers.

In Coast Guard search-and-rescue missions, a third crew member operates the helicopter's hoist equipment. (Aerospatiale)

HH-65A DOLPHIN FACT SHEET

Manufacturer: Aerospatiale

Type: Search and rescue

Power Plant: Two Textron Lycoming LTS 101-750A turboshafts, each producing 680 horsepower

Length: 38 ft., 2 in.

Height: 11 ft., 6.5 in.

Maximum Takeoff Weight: 8,920 lb.

Main Rotor Diameter: 39 ft., 2 in.

Crew: Pilot, copilot, air crewman/hoist operator

First Flight: 1979

Cruising Speed: 160 mph

Range: 470 mi.

Aerospatiale produces a special version of the AS-366 for use in antisubmarine warfare. Such helicopters are equipped with dunking sonar. (Sonar, from *Sound Navigation Ranging*, is a method of detecting and locating objects submerged in the water by means of sound waves the objects reflect or produce.) While hovering, the helicopter lowers a sonar sensor into the water, which allows the aircraft to detect a submarine without being detected itself.

The latest helicopter in the Dauphin family is the AS-565, called the Panther by Aerospatiale. This aircraft made its first flight on February 24, 1984.

While the Panther has the basic layout of the Dauphin 2, there are several differences. The entire airframe has been strengthened, meaning that the crew's chances of surviving are more likely in the event of a crash. The pilot and weapons-system operator sit in armor-plated seats, thus protected from enemy fire. The helicopter's fuel tanks are self-sealing, and the fuel lines have been given added protection.

The Panther's engines provide a maximum speed of 184 mph and a cruising speed of 172 mph. The helicopter has a hovering ceiling of more than a mile—7,546 feet. With its standard fuel tanks, and no extras, the Panther has a range of 460 miles.

Troop transport is one of the chief roles the Panther can be called upon to fill. Its main cabin can accommodate 10 fully equipped troops.

The troop seats can be rapidly removed, folded and stowed inside the aircraft's cargo hold. The hold can also be used to carry an extra fuel tank.

When assigned to support ground troops, the Panther can be fitted with a wide variety of munitions. To attack enemy troops or light vehicles, a rocket launcher is mounted on each side of the Panther's fuselage. Each launcher packs as many as 22 rockets, depending on their size. Instead of a rocket launcher, the Panther can be fitted with 20mm cannons. Whether it has rockets or 20mm shells, the pilot has an electronic sighting and aiming system to be able to fire accurately.

The Panther can also serve as an antitank helicopter. For this role, it carries eight antitank missiles and is also equipped with a tank-sighting system that is operated from the left cockpit seat. The system's optical channel spots tanks during daytime, while an infrared channel is used at night.

Production models of the Panther started to become available in 1988. The aircraft soon gained praise for Aerospatiale and its ability to produce helicopters with a solid, basic design that can be adapted for a variety of missions.

6 BOEING CH-47 CHINOOK

A twin-rotor aircraft, the Chinook saw duty in the Persian Gulf, performing all types of heavy lifting tasks. (Boeing)

In the war in the Persian Gulf early in 1991, the allies smashed the Iraqi Army with a mammoth air-ground assault. In less than 100 hours, the tiny nation of Kuwait was liberated and all of the allied military objectives were met.

The strategy used by allied forces was hailed for its brilliance. During the early morning hours of February 23, Saudi troops and U.S. Marines

launched a headlong attack into the very tough Iraqi barrier system of barbed wire and minefields. But this was merely a feint, a bit of fakery, meant to get the enemy thinking it was the main assault.

In the days before, U.S., British and French forces—close to 250,000 troops, thousands of tanks and mountains of supplies—had been hauled 50 miles to the northwest along Iraq's undefended border. Because its Air Force had been wiped out, Iraq was unable to detect the bold flanking maneuver.

These forces led the "real" ground assault into Iraq and Kuwait, taking the Iraqis by surprise. Many of Iraq's guns were pointed in the wrong direction. Many Iraqi tanks were shot from the rear.

An enormous convoy of trailer trucks was used in "leapfrogging"the troops, tanks and supplies to the jumping-off point. The roads to the staging area were bumper-to-bumper day and night.

But the operation might not have been successful had it not been for the role played by helicopter transports, and by CH-47D Chinooks in particular. Giant bladders of fuel slung beneath scores of Chinooks were used to establish a major fuel depot for allied tanks and armored vehicles. "A truck stop behind enemy lines," was what *Newsweek* called it.

Battlefield heroics were nothing new for the CH-47 Chinook. During the war in Vietnam, the CH-47 was one of the Army's key transportation vehicles. It delivered big loads of troops and cargo of every imaginable type to remote landing strips and hot spots under fire. With the lowest accident rate of all aircraft that served in Vietnam, the Chinook won a reputation for dependability unmatched by any other helicopter. It played a vital role.

The story of the CH-47 Chinook goes back to the late 1950s, when the U.S. Army was seeking a helicopter to replace its CH-21, CH-34 and CH-37 troop carriers. The Army asked several manufacturers to submit designs for the new aircraft.

The winning design was presented by Vertol Aircraft (which had merged with Boeing to become Boeing/Vertol). In July 1958, the Army ordered ten prototypes.

Flight-tested during the late 1950s and early 1960s, the new aircraft had most of the same features as today's CH-47D. It was a twin-rotor aircraft, with the rotor blades mounted on vertical pylons at the front and rear of the aircraft. It had a box-shaped, watertight fuselage. The fuel tanks, electrical systems and such were housed in long pods that ran the length of the fuselage on both sides. This provided for much more storage space inside the cabin.

CH-47D FACT SHEET

Manufacturer: Boeing Helicopters

Type: Medium-lift multipurpose helicopter

Power Plant: Two Lycoming T55-L-712 turboshafts, each delivering 3,750 horsepower

Length: 50 ft., 9 in.

Height: 18 ft., 7 1/2 in.

Maximum Takeoff Weight: 46,000 lb.

Main Rotor Diameter: 60 ft.

Crew: (3) Two pilots, one crew chief

First Flight: 1968

Cruising Speed: 170 mph

Range: 300 mi.

In a twin-rotor helicopter such as the Chinook, the rear rotor overlaps the front rotor. One rotor turns in a clockwise direction, the other, counterclockwise. As a result, the torque generated by one rotor neutralizes the torque generated by the other. This eliminates the need for a tail rotor.

The pilot, when tilting the control column to the right or left, tilts both rotors. Forward- or back-tilting decreases one rotor's pitch while increasing the pitch of the other. This movement causes the aircraft to dive or climb.

The rudder pedals enable the pilot to swing the nose of the helicopter to the right or left by simultaneously tilting the forward rotor blades to the right and the rear rotor blades to the left and vice versa.

At the time the CH-47 was being tested, the war in Vietnam was getting hotter. The Army hurried the test flights in an effort to get the helicopter into production sooner. At about the same time the Army ordered the first production models, the aircraft was assigned the name Chinook (after a tribe of North American Indians that once inhabited the Columbia River basin in Oregon).

The first production models of the CH-47A were delivered to the Army in 1962. At the time, military strategy in Vietnam was going through a period of drastic change. "Air mobility" was becoming the order of the day. A study of battlefield situations recommended the forming of complete air-assault divisions. The combat troops who made up these divisions were to be transported by helicopters instead of land vehicles. They were to be equipped with weapons that were light in weight and supported by aircraft-mounted rockets instead of heavy artillery.

In January 1964, the concept of air mobility was field-tested in maneuvers that took place on a wide stretch of land extending from Fayetteville, North Carolina to Columbia, South Carolina. There the Army's crack 82nd Airborne Division was pitted against an air-assault division that had been formed by Maj. Gen. W. O. Kinnard, who had long championed the use of the helicopters in transporting ground troops.

Although Kinnard's forces were hampered by bad weather, their mobility enabled them to fight successfully on several fronts at the same time, while covering an unusually large area. As a result, on July 28, 1965, President Lyndon B. Johnson announced he was ordering the newly-formed First Cavalry Armored Division to Vietnam. Nick-named the "Flying Horsemen," the 16,000-strong division and its 428 helicopters reached Vietnam that summer.

The Chinooks first saw action in Vietnam about this time, late in 1965. They quickly proved to be both dependable and very adaptable. Time after time, they hauled enormous loads into hostile areas, often under heavy fire and in the worst of flying conditions. So successful was the CH-47 that the Department of Defense ordered production of the aircraft doubled to meet the increased demand.

While the Chinook was intended chiefly as a troop carrier, it was seldom used in that role. That mission was undertaken by the UH-1 Huey, which was smaller and more maneuverable.

The Chinook was used for artillery movement and heavy supply lifts. It did not entirely abandon transporting troops, however. And when it did ferry troops into combat, it did it in a big way. Lifts hauling up to 75 South Vietnamese soldiers on a single flight were not uncommon.

During its Vietnam service, the CH-47 normally carried a crew of three: a pilot, copilot and flight engineer, who also served as a gunner. The standard armament consisted of two 7.62mm machine guns. One was mounted in the opening of an escape hatch on the left side of the aircraft. The other was fitted to a swing-out mounting in the doorway of the crew's entrance to the plane, on the right side of the helicopter. Both guns were provided with a mechanical stop that worked to prevent the gunners from mistakenly firing into the rotor or fuselage during the fury of battle. When the Chinook served as a transport, crew members removed many of the cabin windows to allow troops to fire their rifles at the enemy.

The CH-47 was often employed to place artillery pieces atop mountain positions that could not be reached by any other means. Once the artillery battery and crew were in place, CH-47s kept the base resupplied with food and ammunition. Troops in the field had a nickname for the CH-47; they called it the "Hook."

Another important mission assigned to the CH-47 was the recovery of downed aircraft. In fact, the CH-47 became the Army's chief recovery helicopter in Vietnam. During the course of the war, the Chinook was credited with the recovery of more than 11,000 aircraft worth several billion dollars.

The Army's prime mover, a CH-47D transports massive quantities of fuel in huge doughnut-shaped rubber bladders. (Boeing)

"Hook"s also played a crucial role in supplying fuel to tanks and armored vehicles in remote areas. In such operations, the fuel was loaded into 500-gallon rubberized fuel cells, each weighing 3,500 pounds. These were carried as underslung cargo, suspended from one of the CH-47's cargo hooks.

The Chinook was also used for medical evacuation and paratroop drops. During the battle to retake the city of Hue in 1968, Chinooks were used to supply the battle zone from cargo ships offshore. This is believed to be the first ship-to-shore combat supply effort in U.S. Army history.

In delivering troops to combat areas, CH-47s sometimes unloaded the soldiers by means of rope ladders that were suspended from the aircraft's rear cargo ramp. Such operations were a true test of the pilot's skill, for they required hovering for a relatively long period of time, often in a hostile area and under fire.

The CH-47 was even used as a "bomber." In Binh Dinh province, the Viet Cong had built an extensive system of tunnels, which they used as protection against American and South Vietnamese guns and bombs. They could withstand almost anything but a direct hit.

In their frustration, the Army decided to try tear gas to drive the enemy from their underground hideaways. Chinooks were used to deliver the chemical agent, which was loaded into standard 55-gallon metal drums. Each drum was armed with a fusing system which automatically exploded at a preset distance from the aircraft. Once over the target area, the crew members simply rolled the drum off the CH-47's cargo ramp.

During the same operation, Chinooks also dropped drums filled with napalm, a highly inflammable, jellylike substance. A single CH-47 could drop two-and-one-half tons of napalm on a single mission.

In the mid-1960s, the Army began looking for a heavy-duty helicopter gunship—one with greater firepower and range than Bell's AH-1G HueyCobra. One suggestion was to modify the CH-47 for the role, fitting out the aircraft with a mix of manned gun turrets, grenade launchers, cannons and rockets. Armor protection for the crew would also be provided.

Early in 1966, after extensive testing of a prototype, three production aircraft were delivered to the Army. By May that year, these three Chinook gunships, plus the prototype, were in Vietnam and ready for testing in combat.

Fully loaded, the new aircraft was not very fast, having an airspeed of from 130 to 135 miles an hour. It carried fuel enough to handle missions of up to two hours' duration. It was meant to be manned by a crew of eight, most of them gunners.

As part of its conversion to a gunship, the CH-47 was fitted out with armored seats for the pilot and copilot. These were capable of withstanding hits from shells up to .50-caliber in size. More than a ton of armor was added to the airframe, including armor plate that was installed to the airframe, including armor plate that was installed beneath the aircraft's nose and attached to the rotor pylons. In effect, the CH-47 had become a flying battleship.

The unusual aircraft was fitted with small stub wings on each side of the fuselage. A 20mm gun was mounted on each of the wings. Some 800 rounds of ammunition for the guns was stored in the fuselage. Rocket pods and minigun pods were slung beneath the wings. A 4mm grenade launcher was placed in a turret beneath the aircraft's nose.

Within the aircraft, special mounts were installed at five positions for .50-caliber machine guns. Each gun was provided with 4,000 rounds of ammunition.

When tried in combat, the Chinook gunships produced mixed results. Thanks to their enormous firepower, they quickly put out of action any enemy stronghold they attacked. Troops supported by the gunships loved them. Wherever they were used, they boosted morale.

But in the air, the CH-47 gunships were lumbering targets, ungraceful and relatively slow-moving. They required much more maintenance than the standard CH-47s. Because of battle damage and accidents, three of the four Chinook gunships were lost by January 1967. The Army then decided to end the experiment.

Chinooks flew 2.6 million sorties during the war in Vietnam, compiling 1,182,000 flight hours. They transported 8 1/2 million passengers and 4 1/2 million tons of cargo. A total of 170 Chinooks were lost during the war, either during combat operations or as a result of accidents. Since there were only 732 CH-47As, Bs and Cs produced in all, that means that almost one Chinook out of every four ended up as a casualty.

The Army's latest version of the Chinook is the CH-47D. Delivery of the first production models began in 1983, with the first examples of the new aircraft going to the 159th Assault Helicopter Battalion, 101st Airborne Division, at Fort Campbell, Kentucky.

The Army will eventually operate a fleet of 518 CH-47Ds. This armada will include 436 modernized CH-47As, Bs and Cs, plus 82 new aircraft. In the modernization program, each aircraft is stripped down to the airframe, then fitted out with state-of-the-art equipment and avionics. The modernization is so thorough that each aircraft that has gone through the program not only is redesignated a CH-47D, it also gets a new serial number.

The CH-47D is powered by a pair of Lycoming engines, each producing 3,750 horsepower. The fiberglass rotor blades are 60 feet in diameter, the same as those on the CH-47C. But the CH-47D's blades have a 32-inch chord, as compared to a 24-inch chord on the CH-47C. (The chord is the straight-line distance from the leading edge to the trailing edge of a blade.) The greater chord distance produces much greater lift as well as increased maneuverability.

Other features of the CH-47D are an automatic flight-control system and improved electrical and hydraulic systems. Also included are armored crew seats and crash-resistant fuel lines and tanks.

The spacious cabin of the CH-47D can carry as many as 44 combat-ready troops, or other payloads amounting to 48,000 pounds. It can haul "sling" loads at speeds of 120 miles an hour. The aircraft boasts a triple-hook arrangement, meaning it can carry three different sling loads, each possibly with a different destination.

The CH-47D was the first helicopter of its size able to lift the Army's 155mm howitzer, its crew of 11, and 32 rounds of ammunition on a single mission. To accomplish the same mission in earlier days, two CH-47Cs would have been required.

The aircraft has a maximum speed of 185 miles an hour and a cruising speed of 160 miles per hour. It can climb at a speed of 3,130 feet per minute and hover at 17,000 feet.

Moving troops, artillery and special weapons is only part of the Chinook's mission. It also is counted on to transport fuel and ammunition and to repair parts. The Army expects the CH-47D Chinook to continue to provide these battlefield support duties into the late 1990s and perhaps even beyond.

7   SIKORSKY CH-53E SUPER STALLION

The CH-53E Super Stallion is the largest and most powerful helicopter in the world. Designed by Sikorsky Aircraft for use by the U.S. Marine Corps, the huge, three-engine aircraft is capable of some unusual lifting feats.

The Super Stallion can carry a 155mm howitzer (a short-barreled cannon) and its ammunition in an underslung load. The howitzer's crew rides in the cabin.

CH-53E SUPER STALLION FACT SHEET

Manufacturer: Sikorsky Aircraft

Type: Heavy-duty multi-purpose helicopter

Power Plant: Three General Electric T64-GE-416 turboshafts, each delivering 4,380 horsepower

Length: 99 ft., 1/2 in.

Height: 28 ft., 4 in.

Maximum Takeoff Weight: 73,500 lb.

Main Rotor Diameter: 79 ft.

Crew: (3) Two pilots, one crewmember

First Flight: 1974

Cruising Speed: 175 mph

Range: 1,290 mi.

A Navy MH-53 Sea Dragon tows a sea sled designed to explode magnetic or acoustic mines. (Sikorsky Aircraft)

The aircraft is also capable of carrying another (empty) CH-53E, also in an underslung position. One of the Super Stallion's chief tasks is to serve as a recovery "crane,"picking up damaged aircraft from a carrier's deck.

Four CH-53Es can whisk more than 300 Marines into battle in a two-wave lift, 54 and even more soldiers and their field guns in each helicopter on each wave. Used primarily by the Marine Corps but also by the Navy, the Super Stallion has been on active duty since 1983.

The Navy version of the aircraft, designated the MH-53E Sea Dragon, is a minesweeping helicopter. It is designed to detect and destroy mines of all kinds—acoustic (those that react to the sound of a ship's engines or propellers), magnetic or mechanical.

Sometimes the Sea Dragon will tow a sledlike device over the surface of the water in an effort to explode magnetic or acoustic mines. Other times, the helicopter will set off explosive charges that are intended to cut the moorings attaching certain types of mines to the seabed. When the mines bob to the surface, they are exploded by gunfire from surface ships.

The MH-53E Sea Dragon and CH-53A Sea Super Stallion are the latest in a long line of large helicopters manufactured by Sikorsky Aircraft that go back to 1959. These include the RH-53 A/D and CH-3 A/D, both of which were known as the Sea Stallion.

The first Marine Corps CH-53A Sea Stallions went to war in Vietnam in 1967. At the time, the aircraft represented a giant step forward. Equipped with two General Electric turboshaft engines, each delivering 3,080 horsepower, the Sea Stallion had a lifting capability of more than 18,000 pounds, or more than four times that of the UH-34, the piston-engine helicopter that the CH-53A replaced.

The U.S. Air Force used a modified version of the CH-53A for search-and-rescue operations in Vietnam. While its speed was about the same as the Marine Corps' aircraft, its range was increased by some 650 to 700 miles with the installation of auxiliary fuel tanks. Operating from Udorn, Thailand and Da Nang, South Vietnam, the helicopter could reach any point in North Vietnam and still have enough fuel to get back to its base in the South.

The Air Force designated its aircraft the HH-3E. It came to be nicknamed the Jolly Green Giant.

In 1967, the Air Force got its first deliveries of the CH-53C. Larger than the CH-53A, it could transport 38 passengers more than 260 miles without the need for auxiliary fuel tanks. For protection, it had three 7.62mm miniguns. It earned the nickname Super Jolly Green Giant.

Night rescues were a big problem for Air Force search-and-rescue helicopter teams until 1971. That year low-light-level television equipment that allowed pilots to "see" in the dark became available for the first time. This equipment helped immediately in boosting the number of night-time rescues.

Air Force helicopter rescue teams compiled an outstanding record during the war in Vietnam. Between 1964 and mid-August 1973, they helped to save 3,883 lives. About 70 percent of those rescued were American military personnel.

But the rescuers paid a high price. During the war, 71 American rescue crewmembers were killed and 45 rescue aircraft were destroyed.

In early 1975, when the end of the war finally came in Vietnam, with the South Vietnamese crumbling under the guns of the North Vietnamese, Marine Corps CH-53s and CH-46s were there. They evacuated Americans from Saigon, the South Vietnamese capital, until the very end. U.S. Ambassador Graham Martin was one of the approximately 2,000 men and women rescued in the war's final days.

Through the years, different models of the CH-53 Sea Stallion were involved in a number of major rescue missions. All were very risky. None could be called truly successful, and one was a complete disaster.

In May 1975, the *Mayaguez*, a small American merchant ship headed for Thailand, was seized by a Cambodian gunboat in the Gulf of Siam.

The CH-53E Sea Stallion performs a wide range of heavy lifting chores for the Marine Corps. (Sikorsky Aircraft)

President Gerald Ford ordered an assault operation to free the 39 members of the ship's crew, believed to be held on Koh Tang, an island off Cambodia.

Before dawn on the morning of May 15, eight CH-53s took off from U Tapao to attack Koh Tang. One of the CH-53s crashed because of mechanical failure, bringing death to all 23 passengers and crew members. Cambodians defending the island shot or badly damaged five other CH-53s.

Three CH-53s eventually landed their troops on the island, and three other helicopters put Marines aboard the American destroyer escort *Holt*, from which they boarded the *Mayaguez*. Cambodia surrendered the ship and freed the crewmembers. But the cost was heavy: 41 American service personnel died and 50 were wounded.

The next time helicopters were used in a rescue attempt, the results again were tragic. And the operation did not produce even a hint of success.

The mission took place during Jimmy Carter's presidency and was ordered by him. Carter had won wide praise for the role he had played in peace negotiations between Israel and Egypt. But this success was all but forgotten when militant Iranian students seized the American embassy in Teheran on November 4, 1979, and took 90 men and women, including 66 Americans (of whom 13 were soon released). The students demanded the return of Shah Mohammed Riza Pahlavi, who was undergoing medical treatment in New York.

President Carter used diplomatic efforts to try to get back the hostages. But nothing worked. As the weeks turned into months, Carter lost his patience. A military rescue mission seemed to offer a quick solution.

American military experts drew up a complicated two-phase plan to pluck the hostages from the embassy. On April 24, 1980, the plan was set into motion.

In Phase 1 of the plan, six huge C-130 Hercules cargo planes carrying a total of 90 commandos, an all-volunteer group drawn from the four services, took off from an airfield in Egypt. Their destination was a remote landing strip in the Iranian desert southeast of the Iranian capital of Teheran. At the landing strip, the C-130s were to meet eight RB-53D Sea Stallions from the carrier *Nimitz* in the Arabian Sea.

Phase 2 called for the RB-53Ds to ferry the commandos to a mountain hideaway some 100 miles from Teheran. There the troops were to remain in hiding through most of the next day.

As darkness fell, the commandos were to board trucks and buses for the trip to Teheran. These vehicles were to be provided by CIA (Central Intelligence Agency) agents and other persons working for the Americans, some of whom had entered Iran disguised as businessmen. The vehicles were to slip into Teheran one by one, meeting at a warehouse that had been acquired by an American agent.

Once the actual assault was launched, the commandos were to scale the embassy walls, kill or capture the guards, and release the hostages. The eight helicopters, meanwhile, would have flown to Teheran and landed on the embassy's soccer field, where they would await the arrival of the commandos and the freed prisoners. The helicopters would then take off and rejoin the C-130 transports at the secret desert airstrip. The plan also called for the helicopters to be abandoned at the airstrip, with everyone being flown to safety in the transports.

There was no problem with the C-130s. One by one the big planes made their way to the secret airstrip and landed without incident.

With the helicopters, however, nothing seemed to go smoothly. After taking off from the carrier *Nimitz*, two of the RB-53Ds broke down while flying through a fierce desert sandstorm. On one of the helicopters, the gyrocompass and horizon indicator failed. The pilot flew back to the *Nimitz*.

The second helicopter could not stay aloft because of a hydraulics problem. The pilot had no choice but to make an emergency landing in the desert. Another helicopter spotted the downed aircraft and landed to pick up the crew. As a result of these incidents, only six of the eight helicopters reached the airstrip where they were to rendezvous with the C-130s.

But one of the helicopters arrived in a damaged condition. A pump that powered one of the aircraft's hydraulic systems had broken down. Without that hydraulic system, the helicopter could not fly.

Officers in charge debated whether the mission could be completed with only five helicopters. The original plan had called for a minimum of six. It was decided to scrub the mission.

Before all involved could board the C-130s for the return flight to Egypt, disaster struck. The rotor blade of one of the Sea Stallions sliced into the fuselage of a C-130 parked on the landing strip. Both aircraft were instantly engulfed in flames. Eight American crewmen died in the accident, which added a final note of tragedy to the operation. The commandos and other air crewmen then returned to Egypt aboard the C-130s.

The hostage crisis plagued President Carter until his term of office ended in January 1981. At about the same time that Ronald Reagan, the new President, was concluding his Inaugural Address, the Iranian government released the 53 American captives. They had been held for 444 days.

Political observers have said that the failure of the rescue mission in the desert contributed to President Carter's loss of the election to Ronald Reagan. It made American military leaders look like bumblers, incapable of keeping their aircraft in the air. They could not even prevent them from crashing into one another. It was a great embarrassment for President Carter and all the others involved.

Had either the CH-53E Super Stallion or the MH-53E Sea Dragon been available for the desert rescue mission in 1980, the result might

The U.S. Coast Guard uses the CH-53E as a search-and-rescue aircraft. The Coast Guard's designation for the aircraft is HH-3F. (Sikorsky Aircraft)

have been different. These helicopters represented a big advance over earlier models.

The Marine Corps did not begin taking delivery of the CH-53E Super Stallion until June 16, 1981. The MH-53 Sea Dragon began operational service with the Navy on April 1, 1987.

The concept of the CH-53E goes back to 1973, when the Marine Corps and Navy began to realize they needed a helicopter with far greater lifting capacity than could be provided by the various models of the CH-53 and RH-53 then available. Rather than go back to the drawing board and design a totally new aircraft, military experts felt that the CH-53 itself could be recast as a much more powerful aircraft.

As a result, in May 1973 Sikorsky Aircraft was awarded a contract to develop a three-engine version of the CH-53. Two prototypes were built, the first of which flew for the first time on March 1, 1974, a month ahead of schedule. The first production models of the new aircraft were delivered in the early 1980s.

The chief improvement in the CH-53E was a third General Electric turboshaft engine. One of the basic requirements of the new aircraft was that it be able to lift 32,000 pounds. The third engine was needed in order to be able to get that much weight off the ground.

The helicopter's rotor blades were extended in length by 7 inches in the E model, and the fuselage was made 11 feet longer. The CH-53E was given a probe mounted low on the nose for in-flight refueling. It can also, while hovering, take on fuel from a seagoing vessel, thanks to a second in-flight refueling system.

In 1989, Sikorsky Aircraft noted the H-53 family of aircraft had been in production for 30 years. Thanks to the CH-53E Super Stallion and MH-53E Sea Dragon, the helicopter seems certain to be flying for several decades to come.

8   WESTLAND LYNX (GREAT BRITAIN)

The British Army's version of the Lynx (foreground) is pictured with a British scout helicopter, one of the aircraft it replaced. (Westland Helicopters)

While Westland's Lynx was designed as a multi-purpose helicopter, the fact that it can play many roles has not hampered its effectiveness as a tank-killer. An extremely agile aircraft, it carries a wide variety and large quantity of weapons. The latest models can operate in any kind of flying weather.

WESTLAND (ARMY) LYNX FACT SHEET

Manufacturer: Westland Helicopters Ltd.

Type: General purpose and utility helicopter

Power Plant: Two Rolls Royce Gem 2 turboshafts, each producing 900 horsepower

Length: 39 ft., 6 in.

Height: 12 ft.

Maximum Takeoff Weight: 10,000 lb.

Main Rotor Diameter: 42 ft.

Crew: (2) Pilot and copilot

First Flight: 1971

Cruising Speed: 165 mph

Range: 390 mi.

The Lynx is the product of Westland Helicopter, a British company that has specialized in building helicopter aircraft for more than 30 years. It has long been the principal supplier of helicopters to the British military.

Through the years, Westland has forged strong links with Sikorsky Aircraft of the United States. In fact, some of Westland's battlefield helicopters are based on Sikorsky designs. The Lynx, however, is Westland's own product.

Westland shares the production of the Lynx (the name refers to a type of wildcat) with Aerospatiale, a French company. Westland handles 70 percent of the production works, Aerospatiale 30 percent.

The Lynx prototype first flew on March 27, 1971. Production models of the aircraft began reaching units of the British Army and British Royal Navy toward the end of the 1970s.

The Army Lynx, which is easy to recognize because of its skid undercarriage, is a general purpose and utility helicopter. It can carry troops or provide armed escort for other troop-carrying helicopters. It can also be used as a reconnaissance aircraft, for search and rescue, or to carry out antitank missions.

The pilot and weapons system operator (or gunner) sit side-by-side. The pilot is on the right; the weapons system operator is on the left, operating the sight and other weapons controls.

In the cabin behind the two crewmembers, there's room enough for 10 fully armed troops or three stretcher cases and an attendant. On antitank missions, the cabin houses three gunners and their missiles and launchers.

The Lynx can haul up to 2,000 pounds of cargo. With a sling system, the load can be increased to as much as 3,000 pounds.

As a tank buster, the Lynx is armed with eight TOW (tube-launched, optically-tracked, wire-guided) missiles. Four are carried on outriggers on each side of the aircraft. Eight TOW reloads can be stowed in the cabin, making for a total of 16 on-board "kills," a greater number than on any other helicopter, except the AH-64A Apache. The missiles are aimed by means of a roof-mounted sight.

The Lynx can also be armed with a mine dispenser. This enables the helicopter to lay down a carpet of mines in the path of advancing tanks or armored vehicles.

The Navy version of the Lynx is different from the Army Lynx in several different ways besides its tricycle landing gear. Navy Lynxes are

The Royal Navy's Lynx has a three-wheeled landing system instead of a skid undercarriage, plus electronic gear for submarine detection. (Westland Helicopters)

equipped with nose-mounted radar, which is capable of detecting even small vessels in rough seas. Data from the radar is displayed on a cockpit television screen. The radar can be used in selecting targets for the Skua antiship missile. The Lynx carries as many as four of these weapons.

The aircraft operates from destroyers, frigates and a variety of other surface vessels. To aid in safe landings from the small stern platforms aboard such ships, a special deck lock has been installed in the bottom of the helicopter's fuselage. As the aircraft hovers over the landing platform, the deck lock attaches to crossed metal strips set into the landing platform. The lock holds the helicopter firmly in place until takeoff, when it is released.

To make it easier to stow the helicopter aboard ship, and to save space, the rotor blades can be folded back. The aircraft's tail section can also be folded.

The Lynx is used by the armed services of more than a dozen nations. Represented here are (from top to bottom) the French Navy, Brazilian Navy, Dutch Navy and Britain's Royal Navy.
(Westland Helicopters)

In an antisubmarine role, the Lynx is especially deadly. It carries not only detection equipment and depth charges but also an antisubmarine torpedo.

The Navy Lynx has found a good number of overseas customers. The Army Lynx is not as popular.

In 1982, the Lynx had a chance to demonstrate its effectiveness in battle. The Falkland Islands, a group of some 200 hilly and windswept islands at the bottom of the globe in the South Atlantic, was the scene of the conflict. In 1833, the British established a permanent colony on the Falklands, which lie about 300 miles east of the Strait of Magellan.

The islands are also claimed by Argentina. To the Argentines, they are also known as Las Islas Malvinas.

On April 2, 1982, Argentina, frustrated by its failure to gain control of the Falklands through negotiation, attacked and captured the headquarters of the British Royal Marines on the islands. The British responded by sending a huge task force from Great Britain to the scene. A bitter, bloody 74-day war followed, until the Argentines were forced to surrender.

The war demonstrated the value of high-tech weapons, specifically the French-built Exocet missile. The Argentines used Exocets to sink the destroyer *Sheffield*, a British container ship, and to do significant damage to two other vessels.

The conflict also demonstrated the value of the Sea Harrier, as short-takeoff-and-landing aircraft, or "jump jet," as it is sometimes called. With their ability to maneuver up or down, to the right or left, or forward or back, Sea Harriers battered Argentine combat planes, attacked troop positions, bombed air strips and flew reconnaissance missions. They played an important role in the British victory.

Finally, the Falkland Islands War underscored the value of helicopters in modern warfare. More than 170 helicopters were used in the fighting.

During the third week of the war, a British Wessex-3 helicopter dropped depth charges near the submarine *Santa Fe*. Badly damaged, the submarine headed for the nearest island in an attempt to beach itself. A Wasp helicopter attacked the sub with missiles, while a Lynx dropped a torpedo near the vessel and harassed it with machine-gunfire. The combined attack crippled the submarine, which later sank.

When the destroyer *Sheffield* was hit, helicopters ferried fire-fighting equipment to the scene and rescued crewmembers of the doomed destroyer. Helicopters also carried out antisubmarine missions on practically an around-the-clock basis.

The newest Lynx is the Super Lynx. It has greater range and can carry bigger loads than previous models.
(Westland Helicopters)

Early in May, a pair of Lynx helicopters from the destroyers *Glasgow* and *Coventry*, both armed with air-to-surface missiles, were sent in search of two Argentine patrol boats. One of the helicopters scored two direct hits on a vessel identified as the *Commodore Somellers*, which exploded and sank. Later in the fighting, a Lynx attacked and sank the *Rio Carcacana*, a merchant ship.

When the British landed their main fighting force on the Falklands, on May 21, approximately 80 helicopters helped out. They transported troops and supplies to the battle scene and provided close air support. The fighting ended on June 14 with the surrender of the last Argentine garrison.

During the early 1990s, work on the Lynx continued. Westland unveiled the Super Lynx, an upgraded version of the helicopter. It offers greater range and the ability to carry heavier loads. It also has new avionics and detection gear. While the Super Lynx has been judged to be especially effective as an antitank helicopter, it can perform other tasks as well.

The Lynx had proven very popular with many of the world's helicopter-using nations. The Lynx is flown by the armed forces of Argentina, Belgium, Brazil, Denmark, France, Holland, Norway, Qatar and West Germany. The first production models of the Super Lynx went to South Korea and Portugal.

9   BELL OH-58D KIOWA WARRIOR

It floats like a butterfly; it stings like a bee. It's the Army's OH-58D Kiowa Warrior, one of the most electronically advanced aircraft being flown today. Its job is to locate and track enemy targets, call in helicopter gunships or artillery fire, and then coordinate the attack.

A two-seat, single-engine, single-rotor helicopter aircraft, the Kiowa Warrior has plenty of "sting" to go with its electronic sophistication, including machine guns, rockets and Hellfire missiles. And for its own defense, the aircraft packs Stinger air-to-air missiles.

OH-58D's mast-mounted sight functions something like a submarine's periscope. The pilot doesn't have to expose the entire helicopter when seeking or tracking a target. (Bell Helicopter Textron)

69

OH-58D KIOWA WARRIOR FACT SHEET

Manufacturer: Bell Helicopter Textron

Type: Armed light observation helicopter

Power Plant: One Allison 250-C30R turboshaft, delivering 650 horsepower

Length: 42 ft., 2 in.

Height: 12 ft., 9 1/2 in.

Maximum Takeoff Weight: 4,500 lb.

Crew: (2) One pilot, one copilot/observer

First Flight: 1981

Cruising Speed: 138 mph

Range: 345 mi.

The OH-58D Kiowa is easy to recognize. Atop the main rotor is a mast- mounted sight, a large ball with two big round "eyes." It looks like something from *Star Wars*. In the sight are housed the helicopter's sensing systems.

Operated by the copilot observer in the left seat, the mast-mounted sight searches for targets using both TV and infrared imaging. Since it is perched above the main rotor, it functions somewhat like a submarine's periscope. The helicopter pilot doesn't have to expose the entire aircraft in order to seek and track a target, only the sight itself. The helicopter can remain safely concealed behind the treeline or a manmade structure.

The OH-58D is far more powerful and maneuverable than the early version of the aircraft, the OH-58A Kiowa. There is a minimum of vibration, which aids the pilot in nap-of-the-earth (hugging the ground) flying. Even in winds of up to 40 miles per hour, from any direction, it's possible to keep the helicopter on course. Top forward speed is about 125 miles per hour.

The cockpit has been designed to ease the workload of the crew in what has been described as one of the most demanding missions in Army aviation. Cockpit switches controlling video displays, radio frequencies and sensors are located on the pilot and copilot's hand grips. Five different radios with some 35 pre-programmed frequencies are available.

Small video displays present information from the mast-mounted sight, including thermal imaging and laser ranges.

Late in the 1980s, the Army decided to arm all Kiowas. (The Kiowas were a tribe of Plains Indians that inhabited what are today the states of Colorado, Oklahoma, Kansas, New Mexico and Texas.) An armament rack, which looks like a stub wing, now runs through the fuselage just to the rear of the cabin. To the rack can be attached pods containing Hydra 70mm rockets and two .50-caliber machine guns, each with 500 rounds

Unlike scout helicopters of the past, OH-58D carries a variety of weapons. Here the aircraft fires its 2.75mm rockets. (Bell Helicopter Textron)

of ammunition. The aircraft is also armed with Hellfire air-to-surface missiles or Stinger air-to-air missiles. With the new armament, the Kiowa was given a new name—the Kiowa Warrior.

Today's quick, maneuverable and well-armed scout helicopter bears a fairly close relationship to the observation balloons of the 18th and 19th centuries. The hot-air balloon, first demonstrated in Portugal in 1709, was the first type of lighter-than-air craft in which flight was achieved.

The balloon went to war in 1794. An "aerostier" representing the French artillery service was carried aloft in the balloon *Entreprenant* during the battle of Fleurus in Belgium. Information provided by the aerostier from on high is thought to have helped the French defeat the Austrians. The flight is cited as the first operational use of an aircraft in war.

Balloons were active participants in the United States' Civil War. On April 15, 1861, soon after the first shots were fired, President Abraham Lincoln issued a call for troops. A balloonist named James Allen was among the thousands to volunteer.

Thaddeus Lowe was the most noted of the Civil War balloonists and the first to demonstrate the tactical value of aerial observation. On June 18, 1861, Lowe climbed to a height of 500 feet in the balloon *Enterprise*.

A telegraph operator, Lowe equipped the balloon with a telegraph key, which enabled him to transmit messages to distant points by means of a wire that trailed along the ground. During his flight, Lowe sent a telegraph message to President Lincoln, explaining, "This point of observation commands an area of nearly 50 miles in diameter . . ."

The President was so impressed he asked Lowe to construct an even bigger balloon to increase his range of vision. The result was the balloon *Union*, which Lowe had ready by September 1861.

On September 24 of that year, Lowe made military history. Hanging above the battlefield, Lowe watched Union artillery fire. When the shells missed their target, Lowe transmitted corrections to the gun crew by telegraph. Union generals were so enthusiastic about the innovation that Lowe was asked to provide five additional balloons along with their crews, forming the Balloon Corps of the Army of the Potomac.

Observation balloons again proved their value in America's war with Spain in 1898, and during World War I, which began in Europe in 1914. By that time, of course, radio transmissions and the telephone had replaced the telegram. And during the war, airplanes joined balloons in the sky.

The advantage of the airplane over the balloon on scouting missions was immediately apparent. The observation balloon was tethered to a single position, and what the observer could see was sorely limited. But an airplane could range over an entire battlefield, and even go deep behind enemy lines.

World War II saw further development of aerial scouting with the use of the L-4 Piper Cub, a small, two-seat, single-wing, single-engine aircraft with a cruising speed about the same as that of a Chevrolet—87 miles an hour. What the Piper Cub did was essentially what Thaddeus Lowe did in his balloon—provide for the accurate adjustment of artillery fire. Of course, the Piper Cub has aerial maps, and the crew benefited from binoculars and voice radio.

After World War II, the Stinson L-5 and, later in 1948, the Aeronca L-16 were the Army's principal scout planes. During the Korean War, from 1950 to 1953, these two planes did most of the Army's artillery observation and reconnaissance. They, in turn, were replaced by the Cessna O-1 Bird Dog, which was to be the last of the Army's fixed-wing scout planes.

The Bird Dog pilot searched out targets, marked them, and then directed air strikes. Since it ambled along at around 100 miles an hour, the pilot spotted targets the crew of a lightning-fast jet could easily overlook. One Bird Dog pilot, for instance, used footprints on a mud flat to detect the direction in which enemy troops were headed, then located the force and called in an air strike.

Between June 1950 and October 1954, Cessna delivered 2,426 O-1s to the Army. While the aircraft performed valuable service, it was handicapped by a lack of armor and self-sealing fuel tanks, and its range was short.

The Army started acquiring light helicopters in 1948. While they were able to hover and land almost anywhere, they were not often used for scouting missions. They required too much maintenance and weren't considered nearly as reliable as the O-1 Bird Dog. Those helicopters that did see action in Korea, the Bell H-13 and Hiller H-23, were used mostly for medical evacuation and airlifting equipment and supplies.

In the Vietnam War, it was much different. Hughes' OH-6A, which arrived in 1965, was the first scout helicopter to see service in Vietnam. It was followed four years later by the Bell OH-58A Kiowa. Both helicopters served with distinction until 1973. During the Vietnam years, 3,613 helicopters of both types were delivered to the Army.

The U.S. Navy adapted the easy-to-operate OH-58A for use in basic helicopter flight training. Known as the TH-57A Sea Ranger, the aircraft

TH-57A Sea Rangers fly in formation near the Navy's Pensacola, Florida training base. (U.S. Navy)

has dual controls, one set for the instructor, the other for the trainee. The aircraft can also accommodate two other observer students. The Navy has purchased 40 TH-57As.

Late in 1980, the Army began seeking a new scout helicopter. After the long and difficult Vietnam experience, the Army knew exactly what it wanted.

The new aircraft would have to be able to fly fast while hugging the ground (nap-of-the-earth flight), making use of the terrain to survive. The helicopter would have to be able to locate the enemy and then call in a helicopter gunship or the artillery, a role that would include designating the target with a laser to guide the gunship's missiles. The new scout helicopter would have to be able to perform these tasks during daylight or nighttime hours, in good weather or bad.

On September 21, 1981, after evaluating several designs, the Army announced that Bell's OH-58D best fulfilled their requirements. Five prototypes were ordered, the first of which made its first flight on October 6, 1983.

Delivery of production models began in December 1985. The first OH-58Ds to go to Army units in Europe were delivered by a CA-5A Galaxy in June 1987. The transport managed to get an even dozen Kiowas in its enormous cargo hold.

The advanced electronics of the OH-58D have greatly expanded the role of the scout helicopter. At one time, its job was merely to seek out information about the enemy and guide artillery or air strikes accordingly. Today, it's much different. The scout helicopter orchestrates the battle. It finds targets, tracks them, and then hands them over to AH-64 Apaches or AH-1 Cobras. It performs the same function for the field artillery, which now can be deadly accurate with the very first round.

The U.S. Navy's version of the OH-58 Kiowa Warrior is the TH-57A Sea Ranger, used as a training helicopter. (U.S. Navy)

Military experts call the OH-58D a "force multiplier." It improves the fighting capabilities of gunship helicopters and the artillery. It is good evidence of the Army's commitment to modernization.

10   AGUSTA A-129 MONGOOSE (ITALY)

Originally intended as a light helicopter to perform in an antitank role for the Italian Army, the Agusta A 129 Mongoose soared well beyond the basic requirement. Indeed, by the early 1990s the Mongoose ranked as the only all-weather, day/night antitank helicopter in full production in Western Europe.

The original Agusta company, established by Giovanni Agusta in Italy in 1907, just four years after the Wright brothers had flown at Kitty

A-129 MONGOOSE FACT SHEET

Manufacturer: Agusta S.P.A.

Type: All-weather day/night attack helicopter

Power Plant: Two Rolls Royce Gem 2 Mk 1004D turboshafts, each delivering 825 horsepower

Length: 40 ft., 3 in.

Height: 10 ft., 11 in.

Maximum Takeoff Weight: 9,039 lb.

Main Rotor Diameter: 39 ft., 6 in.

Crew: (2) Pilot, gunner

First Flight: 1983

Cruising Speed: 160 mph

Range: 390 mi.

Hawk, built many experimental aircraft in the early years of aviation. In the years following World War II, the company acquired the rights necessary to produce helicopters originally developed by such American manufacturers as Sikorsky, Bell, McDonnell Douglas and Boeing.

In recent decades, Agusta has become well known and highly regarded for helicopters of its own design. These include the Agusta 190A, which first flew in 1971, a multirole helicopter produced for army, navy and civilian use.

During the 1970s, the Italian army and Ministry of Defense voiced a need for a light antitank helicopter. Agusta set to work designing the aircraft, relying on its experience with the 109A.

Agusta built five A-129 prototypes, the first of which was flown for the first time on September 15, 1983. The aircraft was named the Mangusta (or, in English, Mongoose, which is a slender, long-tailed

Agusta's experience with the 109A, a highly successful utility helicopter of the 1970s (below), was helpful in designing the A-129 Mongoose. (Agusta)

animal common to India and noted for its ability to kill poisonous snakes). The first production models of the aircraft were delivered in 1987.

The Mongoose has many of the standard features of an antitank helicopter. It has a long, thin fuselage, measuring slightly more than 40 feet. The widest point of the aircraft's fuselage is just over 3 feet, which gives the helicopter a relatively small frontal silhouette—a difficult target.

The two-person crew sits one behind the other, with the weapons-systems operator in the front seat, the pilot above and behind him. Both are surrounded by armored panels and are also protected by armored seats.

The crewmembers have a wide field of view, thanks to the helicopter's large side windows. The front windows are angled, reducing the incidence of light reflection, which can serve as a tip-off to an enemy of the helicopter's approach.

The basic mission of the A-129 is to fly up to 100 kilometers (62 miles) to the battlefield, allowing for a flight plan that requires much zigzagging at treetop level. This would probably double the flight's distance.

Upon reaching the battle zone, the Mongoose is expected to linger for 90 or so minutes, with about half of that time spent hovering. Then the helicopter returns to its base, but with enough fuel remaining to provide a safety margin.

To help the Mongoose survive in battle, many of its vital systems have been designed in duplicate or even in triplicate. Should one system be destroyed by enemy fire, the other would carry the load. For example, there are two separate fuel systems. There are three circuits for flight controls and two independent circuits for rotor and wheel braking. There are two control systems for the tail rotor.

The A-129's performance, its flight controls, electronics, and many of its functions are monitored and controlled by an aircraft-management system called the Integrated Multiflex System. IMS divides its duties into seven different subsystems. It displays to the crewmembers the information they need at any given moment on a video display terminal that looks like a small television screen. The system is managed by computer. But for safety's sake, the Agusta has two such computers. Should one fail, the other takes over.

For antitank missions, the Mongoose carries several different types of weapons. These attach to the helicopter's wing pylons. Four standard TOW missiles can be carried on each wing, together with a pod containing seven 2.75-inch air-to-air rockets. Another combination consists of four Hellfire antitank missiles on each wing, plus a 20mm gun pod. No matter which mix is used, the Mongoose packs a deadly punch.

To defend itself against enemy helicopters, the Mongoose can be armed with Stinger or Sidewinder air-to-air missiles. The Sidewinder is mounted to a launch rail that is fitted to the tip of the A-129's stub wing.

Agusta has big plans for the Mongoose. The company intends to produce several different versions of the aircraft, each of which will share the helicopter's basic components.

One of these is to be a navy helicopter. Based on ship or shore, it would support naval vessels or attack those of an enemy. The aircraft would be equipped with nose-mounted radar equipment for electronic counter-measures, including chaff-jamming, that is, dropping countless long strips of aluminum foil to form an electronic cloud that radio and radar signals cannot penetrate. The aircraft's armament would include air-to-ground and sea-skimming missiles.

Another variation of the basic A-129 is a light battlefield-support helicopter. It will combine the Mongoose's rotor system, engines and landing gear with a completely redesigned and larger fuselage. The changes will make for a cabin long enough to accommodate a 10-person

While basically an antitank aircraft, Agusta's A-129 Mongoose can also serve as a troop carrier. (Agusta)

assault team or six stretchers and two medical attendants. The helicopter is to be provided with a chin-mounted gun turret and side- looking radar.

A utility helicopter, the A-129U, is a third variation of the Mongoose being planned. With more powerful engines than the basic Mongoose, it will be somewhat faster and have a greater range. It will be able to carry as many as 12 passengers. Agusta is under contract to supply 200 129Us to an Argentine aircraft company, and some of those will be sold to other Latin American countries.

Yet another version of the Mongoose is an international helicopter, an aircraft that would involve not only Agusta but also helicopter companies in Germany and England. Called the Tonal, this aircraft will be based on the Mongoose's design but will boast state-of-the-art flight controls and communications equipment. It will be able to carry out antitank and scouting roles and also perform anti-helicopter missions.

No one doubts that the A-129 Mongoose will remain one of the Western world's most noteworthy weapons in the years to come.

11 SIKORSKY UH-60 BLACK HAWK

The UH-60 Black Hawk is planned as the Army's frontline utility helicopter of the 1990s and beyond. Designed to carry 11 combat-equipped assault troops plus its crew of three, the aircraft has triggered the development of several variations and an entire family of Navy helicopters. Indeed, since the Vietnam War, no military helicopter has been as heavily ordered and as widely used—it has logged well over one million flight hours. Close to 2,000 Black Hawks are in operation.

UH-60A BLACK HAWK FACT SHEET

Manufacturer: Sikorsky Aircraft

Type: Multi-role utility and assault helicopter

Power Plant: Two T-700-GE-700 turboshaft engines, each delivering 1,620 horsepower

Length: 64 ft., 10 in.

Height: 16 ft., 10 in.

Maximum Takeoff Weight: 20,250 lb.

Main Rotor Diameter: 53 ft., 8 in.

Crew: (3) Pilot, copilot, crew chief

First Flight: 1975

Cruising Speed: 140 mph

Range: 320 mi.

The UH-60A Black Hawk went into service with the Army in 1978. Since then, it has replaced the UH-1D/H Iroquois—the famous Huey—in countless roles. But the Black Hawk's chief mission is troop transport.

Because it offers more cabin space than the Huey, the Black Hawk can transport several more fully-equipped infantry than its predecessor. As a result, it takes only 15 Black Hawks to replace as many as 23 Hueys.

While essentially an assault transport, the UH-60A has several other uses. Thanks to its wide-body design and big cabin doors, it's an excellent aircraft for medical evacuation or supplying troops in the field. It is also used for reconnaissance.

For lift missions, the UH-60A offers a cargo hook that has a load capacity of 8,000 pounds. It can, for example, carry a 105mm howitzer

Currently the most widely used of all military helicopters, the Army's UH-60 Black Hawk can lift loads of up to 8,000 pounds. (Sikorsky Aircraft)

from that hook, while the crew of four and 50 rounds of ammunition for the gun are transported in the cabin. The UH-60A can also transport a Hummer, the armored vehicle that became famous during the Persian Gulf War, plus its crew and its armament.

The UH-60 is of compact design, which means it is an easy aircraft to airlift. One UH-60A can be carried in a C-130 Hercules, two in a C-141 Starlifter, and no less than six in a C-5 Galaxy.

In recent years, the assault role of the Black Hawk has been strengthened with the addition of new equipment. Sikorsky began conducting test firings of the Hellfire antitank missile from a UH-60A in the late 1980s. Today, the Black Hawk is capable of launching Hellfires while in forward, sideways or rearward flight, or while hovering. It can also fire missiles at night, with the pilot wearing night-vision goggles.

While the Black Hawk has the ability to fire laser-guided Hellfires, it can only do so when it is in what Sikorsky calls a "non-autonomous role." This means each missile target must be designated by equipment aboard an OH-58 Kiowa. A ground crew can also select the target for the Black Hawk.

Besides the utility version of the helicopter, the Army operates a Black Hawk that's loaded with electronic-countermeasures (ECM) equipment. Designated the EH-60C, this aircraft's mission is to locate, monitor and jam enemy radar and battlefield communications.

In modern aerial warfare, radar, used to spot an approaching enemy, is as common as guns and bullets. Radar works because electronic signals bounce off objects in much the same way that traffic noise rebounds off walls or buildings. A radar transmitter sends out electronic signals, then "listens" for an echo. The direction of the echo and the elapsed time of transmission are used to determine an object's location. Because it can "see" at night or through clouds, radar is preferred to other sensing systems, such as optical, infrared, acoustical or magnetic.

But radar has a serious failing. Its signal can be detected by the enemy and used to destroy the radar transmitter. A radar beam can be used as a guide for a missile. The hunter becomes the hunted.

That's where jamming and the EH-60C come in. Jamming is a means of defense against being detected by radar. It is perhaps the most common form of ECM.

To jam enemy radar signals, the EH-60C broadcasts loud noise on the same frequency the enemy is using. The aircraft is also capable of chaff-jamming. Flares dropped by the EH-60C disrupt the flight of missile sensors that home in on heat sources.

The first EH-60C was delivered to the Army in 1987. By the beginning of the 1990s, 66 EH-60Cs were in operation.

By 1990, UH-60s of one type or another were serving at Army installations throughout the nation: in Alabama, California, Georgia, Hawaii, Kentucky, Louisiana, Massachusetts, North Carolina, Texas and Virginia. Overseas, the Black Hawk has been deployed by the Army in Germany, Japan, Panama and South Korea.

Late in 1976, at about the same time the U.S. Army selected Sikorsky Aircraft to design and build what was then termed a Utility Tactical Transport Aircraft System—the helicopter that was to become the UH-60A—the Navy also became interested in the aircraft. At the time, the Navy was seeking an antisubmarine helicopter, one

A Navy SH-60B with its parent ship, the guided—missile frigate Crommelin. Note landing pad at vessel's stern. (Sikorsky Aircraft)

While hovering, a Navy SH-60F Ocean Hawk from the carrier Nimitz *tests its "dipping" sonar.* (Sikorsky Aircraft)

that could operate from cruisers, destroyers and frigates. Many officials felt the UH-60A could fulfill that role. After evaluating the aircraft, the Navy ordered five prototypes. The Navy's version of the helicopter was later designated the SH-60B Seahawk.

The Seahawk is different from the Black Hawk in many ways besides its name. The SH-60B has a chin-mounted pod containing electronic-surveillance gear, and pylons on which two torpedoes or auxiliary fuel tanks can be mounted. It is equipped with a rescue hoist, special search radar, and a launcher for sonobuoys, listening devices that are used in the detection of submarines. The helicopter's main rotor blades and the tail rotor can be folded so that the SH-60B can be made more compact for shipboard stowage.

The one hundred or so SH-60Bs operated by the Navy serve aboard "Oliver Hazard Perry"–class frigates, "Spruance"-class and Aegis-equipped destroyers, and "Ticonderoga"-class guided-missile cruisers. Besides detecting and intercepting hostile submarines and surface vessels, the Seahawks are also used for medical evacuation, search and rescue, and other fleet-support missions.

Aboard its aircraft carriers, the Navy operates a modified version of the SH-60B, a helicopter that is designated the SH-60F Ocean Hawk. The SH-60F has the mission of protecting the inner zone of the carrier battle group from submarine attack.

The Ocean Hawk carries special computers, upgraded avionics equipment and dipping sonar. Sonar (from *s*ound *n*avigation and *r*anging) is an electronic system that sends out sound waves and receives the "echo" that bounces back. By analyzing the echo, the sonar operator can determine the location of a submarine or surface vessel.

The *dipping* sonar aboard the SH-60F enables the helicopter to lower a sonar transmitter while hovering. If no sub is detected, the helicopter can raise the transmitter and then move on to another site.

The SH-60F is also equipped with three acoustic torpedoes. These have the ability to automatically home in on the engine noise or any other sound generated by a submarine. Other armament carried by the Ocean Hawk includes surface-to-air missiles.

Search and rescue is a secondary mission assigned the SH-60F. During the launching and recovery of fixed-wing aircraft, the helicopter stands by to provide rescue service in case a pilot is forced to ditch an airplane.

The first Ocean Hawks went into service at the Naval Air Station, North Island, California in 1989. Fleet deployment took place during the 1990s. The first of the seagoing Ocean Hawks arrived aboard the carrier *Nimitz* in 1991.

The HH-60G is a modified version of the SH-60F. Intended to serve with the Naval Reserve, the HH-60H has a mission that is similar to that of the SH-60F, except that the aircraft has been adapted to operate from the decks of cruisers, destroyers and frigates. The aircraft is capable of recovering the four-person crew of a disabled aircraft at a distance of up to almost 300 miles from the helicopter's launch point. The first HH-60H went into service at the Naval Air Station, Point Mugu, California in 1989.

The U.S. Marine Corps also operates the UH-60A. In the fall of 1983, Marine Corps Black Hawks went to war. Their mission involved the tiny island of Grenada, located in the Caribbean Sea about 100 miles north of Trinidad off the coast of Venezuela.

In response to a request from the Organization of Eastern Caribbean States, U.S. Marines and Rangers and a small force from six Caribbean nations invaded Grenada on October 24. It took only a few days to defeat the Grenada militia, a Cuban infantry battalion, and several hundred armed Cuban construction workers.

During the operation, Black Hawks performed about as well as anyone could have hoped. Operating from the amphibious assault ship *Guam*, UH-60As transported troops to landing zones and evacuated trapped Americans, mostly students attending a medical school on the island. One UH-60A was punctured with 29 bullet holes, sustaining hits to the main and tail rotors, the fuel tanks, and a number of important flight instruments, yet the aircraft managed to survive. CH-53 Sea Stallions, CH-46 Sea Knights, AH-1 Cobras and UH-1H Hueys also took part in the operation.

The U.S. Air Force operates close to one hundred UH-60s as rescue helicopters. Known as MH-60G Pave Hawks, these aircraft are equipped with auxiliary fuel tanks and an aerial-refueling probe for in-flight refueling. They also have more sophisticated radar than their

The U.S. Air Force's MH-60G is a search-and-rescue helicopter. (Sikorsky Aircraft)

UH-60A cousins. Some of these aircraft are operated by the Air National Guard and Air Force Reserve units.

The U.S. Coast Guard is yet another branch of the armed services that flies UH-60As. The agency has purchased four Black Hawks and has borrowed another 12 from the Army. They're used in the effort to curb narcotics smuggling.

The UH-60 has proven to be extremely popular with foreign governments. The aircraft is operated by Australia, Brunei, Colombia, Egypt, Japan, Jordan, the Philippines, the People's Republic of China, Saudi Arabia and Turkey.

In light of its ever-increasing use by all branches of the armed services of the United States and the fact that it is in service with foreign nations in every corner of the globe, the UH-60A is emerging as the most popular military helicopter of all time. Sikorsky rightly calls the aircraft the "Huey of the 1990s."

The Coast Guard version of the Black Hawk, designated the HH-60J Jawhawk, is often used to intercept ships and aircraft involved in drug smuggling. (Sikorsky Aircraft)

12 MESSERSCHMITT-BOLKOW-BLOHM (MBB) Bo 105 (PAH-1) (GERMANY)

By most military standards, Germany's MBB Bo 105 is a small helicopter with limited carrying capacity. Except for its range, it is no performance champion. But at low levels, it is a highly maneuverable aircraft, able to dart about like a nervous sparrow. It not only ranks as one of Western Europe's most important helicopters, but it is also regarded as one of the most capable helicopters for its size and weight produced anywhere in the world.

Bo 105 (PAH-1) FACT SHEET

Manufacturer: Messerschmitt-Bolkow-Blohm (MBB)

Type: Multirole light helicopter

Power Plant: Two 313 KW Allison 250-G20B turboshafts, each delivering 400 horsepower

Length: 28 ft., 1 in.

Height: 9 ft., 10 in.

Maximum Takeoff Weight: 5,290 lb.

Main Rotor Diameter: 32 ft., 3 1/2 in.

Crew: (2) Pilot, copilot

First Flight: 1967

Cruising Speed: 150 mph

Range: 360 mi.

Germany's Bo 105, a light helicopter that is capable of playing many roles, has been ordered by 37 nations.
(Messerschmitt-Bolkow-Blohm)

The Messerschmitt-Bolkow-Blohm group was formed in 1969. But the Bo 105's roots go back further than that. The Bolkow Company, with years of experience in helicopter research, began to plan and design the Bo 105 in the early 1960s.

Small and relatively light from the beginning, the aircraft featured two engines, which made for an important safety feature. Should one of the engines become disabled, the aircraft would be capable of operating with the other.

Another innovation was a rotor of unusual design. With most helicopters, the rotor blades are hinged to the hub. But the Bo 105 features a rigid hub; it's hingeless, which helps to prevent the blades from flapping and dragging. This serves to increase the stability of the helicopter and provides for greater maneuverability. It also reduces vibration.

Construction of three Bo 105 prototypes began in 1964. The first flight of one of the prototypes took place on February 16, 1967. The first Bo 105s began rolling off the MBB production line in the early 1970s.

In 1975, the Bo 105 was chosen by the West German minister of defense as the nation's antitank helicopter. (In 1990 East Germany was unified with the Federal Republic of Germany.) This version was designated the PAH-1, which stands for *Panzerabwehrhubschrauber der 1 generation*, that is, antitank helicopter of the 1st generation.

The Bo 105 (PAH-1) carries six HOT missiles, three on each side of the aircraft. (Messerschmitt-Bolkow-Blohm)

The Bo 105 (PAH-1) is somewhat different from the civilian version of the Bo 105. It has a reinforced rotor and strengthened transmission system. It was given a rupture-proof fuel system and a skid landing gear. This enables the aircraft to survive rough landings.

As for its armament, the PAH-1 has been fitted out with the HOT (for high subsonic, optically guided, tube-launched) missile. Produced by Euromissile, a company established by MBB and Aerospatiale, a French helicopter manufacturer, the HOT missile is powerful enough to penetrate even the thickest tank armor. The missile has a range of 13,125 feet and can reach a target at that distance in 17 seconds.

The PAH-1 can carry six HOT missiles, three on each side. In the PAH-1, the weapons systems officer, who sits in the left seat, sights, aims and fires the missiles, using a sighting system that is mounted on the cabin roof. When the gunner is preparing to fire a missile, this placement of the sighting system enables the helicopter to hover behind the tops of trees or other cover, with only the top of the fuselage and rotor visible.

Slightly more than 200 PAH-1s were ordered by the West German military authorities. They were on active duty by the mid-1980s.

In the years that followed, other uses were found for the helicopter. Its missions included observation, armed reconnaissance, and search and rescue. For such missions, the aircraft carried air-to-ground rockets, 20mm cannons or machine-gun pods.

Production of the Bo 105 (PAH-1) continued into the 1990s. More than 1,200 were built. The helicopter's customer list reads like a run-down of United Nations members. As of 1990, 37 nations were flying the aircraft, making it one of Germany's most successful aircraft projects. No one doubts that the Bo 105 will continue in military and civilian service for many years to come.

The Eurocopter Tiger looms as Europe's helicopter of the future. The aircraft was first flown on April 27, 1991. (Messerschmitt-Bolkow-Blohm)

Some of the design features of the Bo 105 (PAH-1) are to be included in one of Europe's most promising military helicopter projects of the future. To be produced jointly by MBB and Aerospatiale, this helicopter will be known as the Eurocopter Tiger. It made its first flight on April 27, 1991. It is scheduled to go on active duty with the German and French military services in 1997.

13 BELL/BOEING V-22 OSPREY

Imagine an aircraft that can hover and fly straight up and straight down like a helicopter, but in level flight has the speed and range of a turboprop airplane. It's an aircraft that doesn't need airports or runways; it can land on a dime.

Such an aircraft is no dream. It's the Bell/Boeing V-22 Osprey, a tilt-rotor plane. It is powered by rotor blades, one on each wingtip. The blades face up for takeoff, landing and vertical flight. By flicking

---

V-22 OSPREY FACT SHEET

Manufacturer: Bell Helicopter Textron and Boeing Helicopters

Type: Advanced vertical lift aircraft

Power Plant: Two Allison T406-AD-400 turboshafts, each delivering 4,400 horsepower

Length: 62 ft., 7 1/2 in.

Height: 17 ft., 7 1/2 in.

Maximum Takeoff Weight: 60,500 lb.

Rotor Diameter: 38 ft.

Crew: (3) Pilot, copilot, crew chief

First Flight: 1989

Cruising Speed: (helicopter mode): 115 mph

Cruising Speed: (fixed-wing mode): 515 mph

Range: 2,000+ mi.

With its rotor blades spinning on a horizontal plane, the V-22 Osprey functions as a helicopter. (Bell/Boeing)

a thumb switch, the pilot can make the rotor tilt forward, and the craft then speeds through the sky like an airplane. Prototypes of the tilt rotor were flown many hundreds of hours during the early 1990s.

The U.S. Marine Corps plans to buy several hundred Ospreys, using them to replace "true" helicopters as troop transports. Carrying 24 fully armed Marines, the V-22 can fly more than 1,000 miles without refueling.

It's not just the Marines who are interested in the aircraft. The Navy believes the Osprey can be valuable in searching out enemy submarines, while the Air Force feels the Osprey can play a role in rescuing downed pilots. The Army thinks of the Osprey as an aircraft that could be used in evacuating the battlefield wounded. The Osprey is also said to offer enormous benefits to civilian aviation.

The Osprey is a compact aircraft. With a fuselage that is 57 feet, 4 inches in length, it is about the size of a Beech 1900, a popular commuter airline plane.

Power for vertical liftoff or high-speed flight comes from two Allison turboshaft engines, each of which can deliver 6,150 horsepower. The engines and their transmissions are housed in cone-shaped nacelles (housings). The nacelles are fitted with hinges that attach to the wing tips. This allows the nacelles to be tilted from the vertical (helicopter mode) to the horizontal (airplane mode).

The V-22 is the first modern weapon system designed from the ground up for use by all four armed services. Most of the V-22s to be acquired by the U.S. government over the next several years will go to the Marine Corps. Here is a rundown:

- U.S. Marine Corps (MV-22A)—With the ability to carry 24 combat-equipped troops or 6,000 pounds of cargo, the MV-22A is intended to serve as an amphibious-troop assault-support aircraft. It has a crew of three, a cruising speed of 288 miles per hour, and a combat range of 460 miles. It is expected that the 552 MV-22s

When in an airplane mode, the V-22's rotors flip forward and the blades spin vertically. (Bell/Boeing)

Armed with missiles and torpedoes, the V-22 could be the Navy's sub-hunter. (Bell/Boeing)

ordered by the Marine Corps will eventually replace the CH-46 Sea Knight and CH-53 Sea Stallion helicopters now in use.

- U.S. Navy (HV-22A)—Combat search and rescue is one of the most demanding of all missions for any aircraft, and that is the primary role the Navy wants the HV-22A to play. The 55 HV-22As ordered by the Navy will be able to operate at 288 miles an hour and will have a range of 530 miles. While the HV-22A will normally be based aboard aircraft carriers, it will also be able to be launched from other types of vessels (as is the case with helicopters).
- U.S. Navy (SV-22A)—There is no greater threat to Navy surface vessels than enemy submarines. To counter this threat, the SV-22A offers a long range plus the ability to hover. Eventually intended to replace the S-3 Viking, a fixed-wing aircraft, the SV-22A will carry submarine sonar and radar, and will be armed with torpedoes and missiles.
- U.S. Air Force (CV-22A)—The long range and vertical-takeoff capabilities of the Osprey are what appeal to the Air Force, which plans to order 55 CV-22s. Each is to be used in transporting 12 special-forces troops or up to 2,990 pounds of cargo on missions of

up to 600 miles. The CV-22A will have a cruising speed of 288 miles per hour.

The tilt-rotor aircraft might also have an important civilian "mission." With its ability to lift off from downtown helipads, aircraft such as the Osprey could help to relieve the crowding and the fierce traffic jams found at most big-city airports.

Its biggest benefit could be in saving travel time for passengers. As Bell Helicopter has pointed out, the time involved in short-distance airline travel is mostly time spent on the ground. At distances of 700 miles, about one-half of the total trip time is spent on the ground. For shorter trips, it's worse. For a distance of 300 miles, about two-thirds of the trip time is spent on the ground. The Osprey, by bypassing airports completely, would drastically reduce traveling time.

For example, an Osprey carrying 39 passengers could take off from a Wall Street heliport in New York City and put down 45 minutes later at a helicopter landing site in Washington, D.C. The aircraft would avoid the long lines of conventional airplanes waiting to take off in New York, and "stacked up" planes waiting to land in Washington. "It would greatly shorten door-to-door trip time," says an official of the Port Authority of New York and New Jersey, the agency that operates the three airports serving New York City.

That's not the only benefit. Any tilt-rotor flight to and from a helicopter landing site—or "vertiport," the term used by Bell Helicopter—frees taxiing, runway and gate space for larger aircraft. In this way, the Osprey could greatly increase airport capacity.

Another advantage of the tilt-rotor aircraft is that it's quieter than a helicopter on takeoff. It's also quieter in general than most fixed-wing aircraft.

The idea for a tilt-rotor aircraft began taking shape in the minds of aeronautical engineers at Bell Helicopter in the late 1940s. They imagined an aircraft that would be able to hover, move sideways and backward, and take off and land vertically as a helicopter does. It would also have the speed and range of a fixed-wing aircraft.

A three-bladed rotor system would rotate on a horizontal plane. Then, for forward flight, the rotor hub would flip forward 90 degrees. The rotor blades would then rotate on a vertical plane in the same way an airplane propeller rotates.

The engineers' ideas were not translated into actual drawings until the early 1950s. In August 1950, the Air Force announced to aircraft manufacturers it was looking for an aircraft with many of the same features as the tilt-rotor. The Air Force called the aircraft a "converti-plane." The competition triggered the design and construction of several unusual airframes. Bell engineers took the opportunity to present plans for their tilt-rotor, which was designated the XV-3.

Thinking the XV-3 might have a future, the Air Force awarded Bell a contract to build two prototypes. The first prototype flew on August 11, 1955.

In its first test flight, the XV-3 merely hovered. But on December 18, 1958, the XV-3 made aviation history by becoming the first tilt-rotor to go from a helicopter mode to an airplane mode.

Flight tests continued for years. The flights were conducted not only by Bell Helicopter test pilots, but also by pilots from the Army, Air Force and the National Aeronautics and Space Administration (NASA).

The XV-3 program continued until 1966. While it showed the tilt-rotor idea was practical, the flight testing also revealed certain failings that would have to be overcome in future designs.

Even before the XV-3 flight tests were completed, the Army had asked Bell to design another vertical-takeoff helicopter airplane. This led to the construction of another tilt-rotor aircraft, the XV-15. Two proto-types were built.

On July 24, 1979, the XV-15 made its first in-flight conversion from a helicopter mode to an airplane mode and back again. On June 17 the following year, the XV-15 set a world's record for a rotorcraft when it reached a speed of 346 miles an hour during level flight. In 1981, the XV-15 completed a California-to-Texas flight, averaging 334 miles an hour.

Test pilots for NASA and the various branches of the armed forces began flying the XV-15. In addition, guest pilots were invited to take over the controls of the unusual aircraft. One was Barry Goldwater, U.S. senator from Arizona. After his flight, Senator Goldwater called the tilt-rotor concept the "biggest advance in aviation in a quarter of a century."

More test and demonstration flights followed. In 1982, the XV-15 underwent shipboard trials aboard the *Tripoli*, an amphibious assault ship operating in the Pacific Ocean. On August 2, 4 and 5 that year, the XV-15 completed 54 takeoffs and landings. In 1983, the XV-15 con-ducted inflight refueling missions. In 1984, the XV-15 was tested in nap-of-the-earth flights at Ft. Rucker, Alabama. Later in the year, the XV-15 demonstrated its ability as a civilian commuter aircraft, complet-ing the trip from Manhattan, N.Y., to Washington, D.C. in 45 minutes.

By this time, the XV-15 had been chosen by the U.S. Department of Defense as an answer to the battlefield aerial mobility needs of the military services. On January 15, 1985, Secretary of the Navy John Lehman named the aircraft the V-22 Osprey. (The Osprey is a large hawk that is noted for its agility, powerful wings and swift flight.)

Production models of the Osprey would be produced by the team of Bell Helicopter Textron (formerly Bell Helicopter) and the Boeing Vertol Company. Bell would be responsible for the wings, the rotor and transmission systems, and the installation and operation of the engines. Boeing's contribution would be the fuselage, the tail assembly, the landing gear, and installation and operation of the plane's avionics.

In 1986, the Navy awarded Bell/Boeing a contract to manufacture six prototypes of the V-22. The first of these made its first flight on March 19, 1989, at Bell's Flight Research Center at Arlington, Texas.

During 1990 and 1991, the prototypes were thoroughly tested. One V-22 completed the aircraft's first cross-country flight, from Arlington, Texas, to Wilmington, Delaware, with a stop to refuel in Atlanta, a

Its rotors almost upright, the V-22 eases toward a tanker plane for aerial refueling. (Bell/Boeing)

distance of 1,392 miles, in 5.2 hours. Another V-22, in a steep dive, reached a speed of 402 miles an hour. In a sling-load test, a V-22 carried a 4,000-pound load at a speed of 203 miles per hour. By mid-1991, five V-22s (one of the prototypes was destroyed in a crash) had accumulated more than 500 flight hours.

One serious problem with the Osprey is money. The 682 Ospreys ordered by the armed services could cost the taxpayers $28 billion. To some, including Secretary of Defense Richard Cheney, that was too much to pay for an aircraft that its critics sometimes regard as little more than a substitute for a "true" helicopter. Nevertheless, Cheney, in mid-1992, agreed to devote $1.5 billion to further develop the aircraft. Despite this vote of confidence, no one doubted the Osprey faced an uncertain future.

AIRCRAFT DESIGNATION SYSTEM

Aircraft of the U.S. Air Force, Army, Navy, Marine Corps and Coast Guard are classified by a coded system of letters and numbers. This includes not only helicopters but also fighters, bombers, gliders, blimps and about every type of vehicle that goes up and stays aloft.

Most designations are made up of two letters, two numbers, and a third letter that follows the numbers. CH-53E (the Super Stallion) and OH-58D (the Kiowa Warrior) are typical.

The first letter in such a grouping indicates the aircraft's mission. C, as in CH-53E, indicates a transport aircraft. O, as in OH-58D, stands for observation.

Here is a complete listing of mission symbols:

SYMBOL	MISSION
A	Attack
B	Bomber
C	Transport
D	Director
E	Special electronic installation
F	Fighter
H	Search and rescue
K	Tanker
L	Cold weather
M	Multimission
O	Observation
P	Patrol
Q	Drone
R	Reconnaissance
S	Antisubmarine

T	Trainer
U	Utility
V	Staff
W	Weather
X	Research

The second letter in the grouping indicates the aircraft's type. H stands for Helicopter.

Here is a complete rundown:

SYMBOL	TYPE
G	Glider
H	Helicopter
S	Spaceplane
V	VTOL/STOL (vertical takeoff and landing or short takeoff and landing)
Z	Lighter than air

The numbers that follow the letters and hyphen are used to indicate the design number. In CH-53E, the 53 indicates the 53rd helicopter design. Sometimes this is called the model number.

The letter that follows the numbers is the series letter. It indicates the number of modifications that have been made in the design. B indicates the second modification in the design, D the fourth modification, and so on.

Once in a while an additional letter is used *before* all the other leters and numbers. This prefix letter indicates a special status the aircraft has.

Here is a complete listing:

SYMBOL	STATUS PREFIX
G	Permanently grounded
J	Special test (temporary)
N	Special test (permanent)
X	Experimental
Y	Prototype
Z	Planning

GLOSSARY

air-to-air missile A weapon that is launched from one airborne aircraft against another.

air-to-ground missile A weapon launched from an airborne aircraft against tanks, armored personnel carriers, troop convoys or ground stations.

air-to-sea missile A weapon that is launched from an aircraft against enemy ships or submarines.

angle of attack The angle, or "pitch," at which the leading edge of the rotor blade meets the surrounding air.

antisubmarine warfare (ASW) To search for and attack enemy submarines.

armed helicopter A standard utility helicopter with machine guns, rocket launchers and other weapons added.

assault transport helicopter A helicopter designed to deliver fully equipped troops to the battlefield.

attack helicopter A helicopter designed to provide direct fire and anti-armor support.

avionics The science and technology of aviation electronics.

chaff Strips of aluminum foil dropped by an aircraft to confuse enemy radar.

chaff jammers A type of electronic-countermeasures equipment that disperses strips of aluminum foil to create false images on enemy radar.

chord On a rotor blade, the straight-line distance from the leading edge to the trailing edge.

collective pitch lever The control lever that regulates blade pitch to make the helicopter climb, hover or descend.

control column The control system that makes a helicopter fly forward, backward or to either side.

downwash The downward rush of air created by the whirling rotor.

electronic countermeasures (ECM) The many techniques used to deceive or disrupt enemy radar or other electronic signals.

fairing A section of the fuselage skin that covers a part, smoothing the fuselage and reducing drag.

fixed-wing aircraft An aircraft with a wing that does not rotate; an airplane.

fuselage The main body of a helicopter, to which the rotor, engines and tail surfaces are attached.

head-up display A vision plate in front of the pilot that displays flight-control information.

jamming A form of electronic countermeasures that consists of broadcasting loud sounds on the same frequency the enemy is using for communication.

leading edge The front edge of a rotor blade.

lift The force that causes a helicopter to overcome the pull of gravity, rise into the air and stay aloft.

lock on Slang term meaning to fix a weapon's sights on a target by electronic means.

main rotor The helicopter's horizontal "wing," comprised of the blades that provide lift.

medevac Medical evacuation of injured troops from a battle zone.

nacelle An engine's housing.

napalm A mixture of chemicals and gasoline in a jelly that is used in incendiary bombs and flame throwers.

payload The total weight of cargo, passengers, weapons, etc., that a helicopter is capable of carrying.

pod A small compartment on the fuselage of a helicopter, housing radar equipment, weapons or fuel.

prototype The original model of an aircraft.

pylon A curved or angular piece of metal that is used to suspend various types of bombs, missiles or fuel pods from an aircraft fuselage or wings.

radome A usually dome-shaped structure housing a radar antenna.

range The maximum distance an aircraft can travel.

reconnaissance The aerial exploration of an area to gather military information.

root The part of the rotor hub that attaches the blades to the hub.

rotor The helicopter's horizontal airfoil or wing.

rotor hub The central part of the rotor that links it to the engine.

skid One of two runners extending from the underside of a helicopter that serve as a landing platform for the aircraft.

sonar An electronic system that uses transmitted sound waves and their echoes for detecting and locating submarines or other submerged objects. The word is an acronym formed from *s*ound *n*avigation *r*anging.

stabilizer The horizontal section at the end of the tail boom that helps the helicopter to remain stable while in flight.

tail rotor The small rotating blades at the end of the tail of a helicopter, designed to counter torque.

tilt rotor An aircraft that can hover and fly straight up and straight down like a helicopter, but which also has the speed of a turbofan airplane in level flight.

torque The turning and thrusting force generated by a helicopter's rotor.

trailing edge The back or rear edge of a rotor blade.

turbojet The simplest type of jet engine. The exhaust gases provide the trust to propel the aircraft through the air.

turboshaft A type of jet engine in which the exhaust gases are used to drive a power turbine. The turbine, in turn, drives the helicopter's rotor shaft.

turret A heavily armored structure within which one or more guns are mounted.

vertiport A landing place for helicopters and other aircraft that hover and fly straight up and straight down, such as the tilt rotor.

ABBREVIATIONS AND ACRONYMS

AFV Armored Fighting Vehicle

AGM Air-to-Ground Missile

ASM Air-to-Surface Missile

ASW Antisubmarine Warfare

ATA Air-to-Air

CPG Copilot/Gunner

ECM Electronic Countermeasures

FLIR Forward Looking Infrared Radar (sensors)

GAO General Accounting Office

HARM High-speed Anti-Radiation Missile

HOT High subsonic, optically guided, tube-launched (missile)

HUD Head-up Display

IMS Integrated Multiflex System

IR Infrared

LLLTV Low Light Level Television

MBT Main Battle Tank

NATO North Atlantic Treaty Organization

NOE Nap of the Earth (flight)

OMG Operational Maneuver Group

PNVS Pilot Night Vision Sensor

RAF Royal Air Force; the air arm of the United Kingdom

RCAF Royal Canadian Air Force

SAM Surface-to-Air Missile

SRR Short Range Recovery

TADS Target Acquisition Designation Sight

TOW Tube-Launched, optically traced, wire-guided (missile)

USAF United States Air Force

USMC United States Marine Corps

INDEX

Page numbers in **boldface** indicate extensive treatment of a topic.
Page numbers in *italic* indicate illustrations and captions.